GHOST STORIES *of* COLORADO

Dan Asfar

LONE
PINE

Lone Pine International Inc.

© 2006 by Lone Pine Publishing International Inc.
First printed in 2006 10 9 8 7 6 5 4 3 2 1
Printed in Canada

The Publisher: Lone Pine Publishing International
Distributed by Lone Pine Publishing
1808 B Street NW, Suite 140
Auburn, WA 98001
USA

Websites: www.lonepinepublishing.com
www.ghostbooks.net

National Library of Canada Cataloguing in Publication Data

Asfar, Dan, 1973-
　　Ghost stories of Colorado / Dan Asfar.

　　ISBN-13: 978-976-8200-20-4
　　ISBN-10: 976-8200-20-0

　　1. Ghosts--Colorado. 2. Legends--Colorado. I. Title.

GR110.C6A83 2006　　398.209788'05　　C2006-903541-5

The stories, folklore and legends in this book are based on the author's collection of sources including individuals whose experiences have led them to believe they have encountered phenomena of some kind or another. They are meant to entertain, and neither the publisher nor the author claims these stories represent fact.

PC: P5

For Nancy Foulds—*Excelsior!*

Contents

Chapter 4: Native Spirits and Unexplained Phenomena

Chapter 5: Modern Mysteries

Ghostly Glossary

Acknowledgments

The nonfiction paranormal genre is generally greeted with its fair share of skepticism. Since the second half of the 19th century, when the study of purported supernatural phenomena began being reported by supposedly objective voices, there has been no shortage of hoaxes, charlatans and false prophets. And yet the genre persists, as old folktales continue to survive and new accounts of inexplicable phenomena emerge.

Every account in this volume is based on purported hauntings set in the state of Colorado. Some are old supernatural folktales retold, while others are based on interviews with individuals claiming to have come face to face with phenomena beyond their understanding. Still others are rooted in tales that have been unearthed by other authors in this genre.

Allow me to begin by acknowledging the invaluable contribution of those whose tales informed and inspired many of the stories in this book. Thanks to the individuals who took the time to share their bizarre experiences. The identities of these witnesses have been protected, and they have been given pseudonyms where they appear in the text.

The research of authors of previously published books has been invaluable to this text. Thanks to F. Dean Sneed, author of *Ghosts of Trinidad and Las Animas County*. As well, Dean's work in *The Phantom Train and Other Ghostly Legends of Colorado* has provided an important collection of primary sources on 19th-century haunts. Thanks, also, to the prolific MaryJoy Martin for her well-researched and well-written works, *Something in the Wind: Spirits Spooks and Sprites of the San Juan* and *Twilight Dwellers: Ghosts, Gases & Goblins of Colorado.* Earl Murray's seminal *Ghosts of the Old West* served as a valuable reference point for the tale of the Snake People. This book owes much to all of your efforts.

Introduction

Colorado. Mythic state of the equally mythic unbridled West. Historical land of gold rushes, silver rushes, rugged ranches, pioneering settlements, far-flung military outposts and the enduring Indian braves who rode against them all. Colorado was born from heady ambition and conflict, pitting men against one another and against the earth they sought to tame and turn to profit. It could be a brutal process, and while so much of the state's current wealth owes much to such early striving, the landscape is also littered with reminders of the casualties of those early days. There are abandoned towns strewn across the former mining sites; there are discontinued rail lines; there are deserted homesteads. And, of course, there are ghosts.

Denver, Colorado Springs, Pueblo…or, for that matter, New York, Hong Kong, London…really, it doesn't matter where you are. Whether we're talking about the American Rockies or the bogs of Ireland, there are sure to be ghosts haunting the landscape. Or, maybe it would be more accurate to say, there are sure to be stories about ghosts haunting the landscape. And there always have been.

As long as people have been putting pen to paper, there have been ghosts in popular storytelling. There are ghosts in Homer's *Iliad*, one of the original narratives of Western civilization. Ghosts make numerous appearances in the plays of William Shakespeare. The storytellers of the 19th century had a seemingly insatiable appetite for ghosts in their fiction. From the novels of Charles Dickens to the poems of John Keats to the short stories of Edgar Allan Poe, there is an overabundance of supernatural material. That's to say nothing of Victorian England's obsession with Spiritualism and the gothic narratives that fueled the popular imagination and gave birth to the undying dead, notably the vampires of Bram Stoker. In recent years, the ongoing fascination has found voice in the seemingly endless popularity of writers like H.P. Lovecraft, Stephen King and Anne Rice. On the big screen, armies of brain-eating corpses appear in countless zombie flicks, and hundreds of horror movies feature restless spirits of the dead.

One of the interesting things about the supernatural in entertainment is how the notion of ghosts says something about who we are as a people. There's no arguing that the dead have always occupied a big place in cultural expression; the inevitably of death and the question of what follows forms one of the biggest questions, or perhaps *the* biggest question regarding the human condition. Cultures near and far, remote and cosmopolitan might be partly understood by the way their religious beliefs and folkloric narratives tackle the notion of the great hereafter.

In the end, ghost stories are so popular because whether we are prone to dwell upon it or not, death concerns us all. And even if one believes that nothing but oblivion follows, it cannot be denied that any culture can be largely defined by the way it approaches the idea of death. What does this say about our contemporary culture, then, that the notion of ghosts is so widely accepted within entertainment, while generally rejected in reality?

If, as most level-headed Americans would likely state, there is no such thing as ghosts, then why do we continue to be so fascinated by them?

No need to worry. The following pages do not attempt to answer such questions. This is a book of ghost stories, nothing more, and it probably goes without saying that you didn't pick it up with hopes of coming to grips with such issues. Yet it must be stated that not one of the tales has hatched from the whimsy of my imagination. All of these stories are said to be true—supernatural accounts told by the people of Colorado, ghostly folklore that has survived the centuries. Some stories are well known, others are more obscure, but each and every one of them is purported to find its roots in fact, rather than fiction. These are Colorado's ghost stories; I can only claim to be a faithful chronicler of some of the haunts in its history and the uncanny experiences of its citizens. It is up to you to decide whether or not to believe.

1
Ghosts of the Wild West

The Headless Mexican

At dusk on a rugged trail in South Park, a teamster was urging his heaving oxen in the quickly fading light. He was hauling lumber to Fairplay, hoping to make it to town before it got too dark, all the while doing his best to keep his mind on the job, to ignore the anxiety growing in his stomach. *Them Mexican boys have been after loot all this time*, he thought to himself as his nervous eyes darted over the darkening shadows in the surrounding pine trees. *Ain't no way they gonna bother a man with a team of oxen driving nothing better than wood up to town. Ain't no way.* Still, his reassurances did little to quell the growing anxiety; he knew full well that no small number of Park County residents would have called him mad for being out at that hour.

It was May 1863, and a disturbing number of dead bodies were turning up on the roads running through South Park and the San Luis Valley. Earlier that month, a man named William Bruce had been found near his sawmill in Fremont County, shot dead on the banks of Hardscrabble Creek. A few days later, a brutally axed body was found bleeding into Little Fountain Creek in El Paso County. The list continued to grow: two men dead in South Park's Red Hills, followed shortly after by another pair in the same region; a solitary cowboy found butchered on his ranch near Colorado City; the bodies of another two men turning up on the road to Cañon City;

and yet another swollen and decomposing corpse partly submerged in the waters of Currant Creek.

Word of the killing spree spread and panic gripped the region. Speculation about the identity of the killer, or killers, ran rampant. Overprotective citizens put extra locks on their doors as whispered rumors of more murders spread across the countryside and into the towns. No one had a clue as to who was doing the killing; the more superstitious minded even began to suggest that the culprit was not of flesh and bone, but was some wrathful Native spirit or a feral monster imbued with a strength and viciousness limited only by imagination. Whatever the case, whether one believed the murders were the act of supernatural forces or were committed by more corporeal culprits, it became generally accepted that it was a good idea to stay off the roads after dark.

"I oughta have my head checked," the teamster muttered to himself, his eyes nervously darting about the trail. "Riskin' my neck for a wagonload of wood and a pocketful of dollars." A twig cracked nearby. There was a rustling in the trees, and he very nearly jumped out of his wagon, only to see a hare dart away. He shook his head, muttered a few silent curses and urged his team on.

The day's last light was a dull glow in the western sky when he heard another sound in the woods in front of him. He had just made out two figures on horses when the crack of a gunshot split the silence of the early evening. There was a muzzle flash from one of the figures in front of him, followed instantly by a sharp blow to the teamster's chest. He jerked back from the violent force as the wind was knocked out of him. One thought screamed in his mind: *I've been shot!*

And yet he was still alive. Instinctively, he lashed at his team of oxen as if they were the ones who had fired at him. "Go. Go!" he croaked. "Faster, you damn beasts!" He got a clear look at the two figures as he and his team raced by, surely going as fast as oxen ever have. They were clearly visible for only a moment, but in that moment were unmistakable: two young Mexican men in wide sombreros with pistols in their hands, which they had cocked and trained on him, about to fire again.

Ducking low in his seat and manically whipping his oxen, the teamster heard two more shots go off. Bullets whistled over his head, one so close that he felt the sharp little gust of the passing slug against his ear. He crested a hill then, and his oxen went pell-mell down a shallow slope, hauling faster than he ever thought possible, leaving the two Mexican gunmen behind him. He did not stop until he reached Fairplay.

There, in the center of town, the foaming oxen and terrified driver quickly drew an audience. He shouted his first words through ragged breaths. "They shot me!"

The assembled crowd reacted quickly, helping the teamster down from the wagon and calling for a doctor. The wounded man continued to speak as the townsfolk laid him down. "Two Mexicans by the road," he gasped. "Got the jump on me. Didn't ask any questions. Shot me through the chest."

The Fairplay doctor had arrived by then and was examining the teamster's chest. "Where did you take it?" he asked, looking for the wound under the man's strangely bloodless jacket.

"Right here," the man gasped, pointing to a spot over his heart.

The doctor looked to where the teamster was pointing, and there, sure enough, a bullet hole had torn through. And yet, there was no blood. Pulling open the jacket, the doctor immediately solved the mystery of the bloodless wound. In the inside pocket of the man's jacket was President Abraham Lincoln's recently printed Emancipation Proclamation, along with a book of memos. Embedded in these documents was the bullet, stopped short by the papers without piercing the man's chest. He had felt the impact of the bullet, but had been spared the worst.

The teamster lived and brought word of his attackers, who were instantly linked to the plague of murders that had recently sprung up. The two Mexicans were even given names. It was said they were none other than the Espinosa brothers, infamous highwaymen from south of the border who had murdered two men in Santa Fe and a soldier in Conejos on their way north from the state of Chihuahua.

Now that there was a visual description to go on, a posse of 17 volunteers was put together by Captain John McCannon with the goal of bringing these two Mexicans to justice—one way or another. And so began the search for the Espinosa brothers, a prolonged manhunt that took McCannon's posse up and down South Park until they stumbled on the Mexicans' trail along Four Mile Creek, southwest of Colorado Springs. They followed the trail through a rocky gorge on to High Creek and then to a little meadow, where, finally, two horses came into view.

The whispered word went down the line that they had come upon the Mexicans' horses, and the posse dismounted quietly, hiding among the trees and boulders at the edge of the clearing. McCannon hissed at four of his men to creep around to the other side of the meadow so that they would have all the open ground covered. They did not have to wait for long.

There was a stirring in the trees, and then a man emerged, a big man with coarse black hair and a big sombrero, heading over to untie one of the mounts. It had been a long hunt, and now, with one of their targets in sight, McCannon's posse proved unable to hold their fire until the other Espinosa appeared. The first man to shoot hit the Mexican in the chest, and a hail of bullets fell on the lone man in the next instant, leaving him and his horse dead in the clearing. As for the other brother, he had emerged from the forest when his brother had come under attack and would have surely been shot down then and there if it was not for the fact that, from a distance, he looked identical to Billy Young, one of the men riding in the posse.

Every man there trained his rifled on him when he appeared at the edge of the clearing, and then, seeing who they swore was Billy Young, just as quickly jerked their guns away. One man who kept aim long enough to raise a doubt had his gun knocked aside for him. "What the hell you up thinkin' about?!" came the furious voice. "You intend to kill Billy Young?" And so the other Espinosa got away, lunging back into the trees and throwing himself over the lip of a wooded gorge. By the time the posse realized their error, he had disappeared in the dense forest below.

Slinging the dead brother over one of their horses, McCannon's men then made a quick search of the Espinosas' camp, where they discovered evidence that confirmed they were on the right track. Stacks of money, bracelets, rings, watches and other pieces of jewelry were found among bloodstained implements of grisly murder—a heavy butcher knife and a battered and notched ax. In the back pocket of the dead Espinosa was a list of 32 names. They recognized those at the bottom as belonging to the recently murdered Colorado men. "Sweet Jesus," one of McCannon's riders muttered at the long list. "They gone and killed that many?"

"This was more'n about money," McCannon lent his gruff assent. "Killing this many, writin' their names down. There was joy in this thing."

If not joy, at least a sense of mission. They also found a prayer book on the dead man's person—a prayer book covered with insane religious rants, justifying the rampant killing spree the two brothers were on. According to the manic words scribbled across the back cover, the brothers' bloody massacres had the sanction of the whole pantheon of Catholic saints, including the Virgin Mary to boot.

Thankful as the locals were that such a man was no longer conducting his murderous business, the fact that his partner was still at large did little for anyone's peace of mind. Learning of the events near High Creek, the governor got together with a number of the Colorado victims' relatives and put up a bounty of $1500 for the remaining brother's head.

For his part, the surviving Espinosa was undaunted by the demise of his brother. Retreating to New Mexico, he did not allow too many suns to set before recruiting his nephew as his new partner, returning to Colorado soon after to resume his murdering and thieving. For the next few months, they turned South Park and the San Luis Valley into their hunting grounds, setting upon anyone they felt they could take. In the end, however, Espinosa's return made things easier for the bounty hunters. Or, it should be said, for the Colorado mountaineer who ended up with the Mexicans in his rifle sights.

Tom Tobins was a long-time resident of the San Luis Valley who knew every grove, hill and creek there. He was also a hell of a hunter whose sympathies lay firmly with law and order, and he did not hesitate a bit when Espinosa reemerged around the places he was so familiar with. There was $1500 to be earned, after all, the collection of which fit so well with his moral code.

Tobins would not make the same mistake as McCannon's posse. When he saw the thin line of smoke rising from the trees, he went quickly and quietly, rifle cocked, hunched low on the balls of his feet. Sneaking up on the men as they were camped in a small clearing, he moved forward flat on his belly, aimed, and with a hunter's proficiency, killed them both—each with a single bullet through the heart.

Tobins may as well have just bagged himself a couple of deer, for the nonchalance, the practical indifference, with which he strode out from the cover of the trees, pulled out his hunting knife and, without a pause or a flinch, cut off the Espinosa brother's head. He took his dripping trophy as grisly proof of the deed, put it into a satchel and headed back to Fort Garland to collect his money. It ended up taking three decades for the Colorado authorities to cough up Tobins' reward; Espinosa's dismembered head would travel much faster.

After identifying the head, the fort physician, a man named Dr. Waggoner, was, for whatever reason, eager to take the Mexican's head into his possession. Not surprisingly, he was not confronted by anyone with a competing interest, and he was allowed to do what he pleased with the killer's rapidly decomposing head. So he put it into a glass jar filled with alcohol and kept it on his desk as a keepsake. Doctor though he may have been, nowhere in the stories does it mention that Dr. Waggoner was in possession of anything close to a full deck.

When his tenure at Fort Garland expired, Dr. Waggoner took Espinosa's head and, along with the rest of his belongings, packed it into his wagon and departed north for the town of Pueblo. It was while he was crossing over the Sangre de Cristo Pass that his horses suddenly began bucking and rearing for no apparent reason. The doctor clutched the reins in mortal fear as his wagon violently jolted behind him, depositing a good number of his possessions on the trail, among them the jar containing the pickled head. It broke as it fell, sending the late Espinosa's head tumbling down the rock-strewn path. The face split open as it fell, tearing upon jagged, pointed rocks. Stopping the wagon to retrieve his belongings, Dr. Waggoner did not fail to pick up Espinosa's head.

Lacerated and deformed as it may have become, there still would have been some value in the skull. In fact, for most men in Dr. Waggoner's profession, the skull, rather than the pickled face, would have merited far more scientific curiosity. Or, given the way modern medicine has progressed, it might be more accurate to say *pseudo-scientific* curiosity.

For if the reader recalls, it was the 1860s, a time when all sorts of bizarre medical theories were still in wide circulation. One of these was called "phrenology," the belief that certain human behaviors, or tendencies, might be determined by the shape of a person's skull. So it was that human skulls were in high demand among medical professionals, especially if a certain skull once belonged to an individual possessed of an extreme disposition. Espinosa was definitely such an individual. An adherent to phrenology might make all sorts of conclusions based on the bumps and ridges in the Mexican's skull.

So it was that Dr. Waggoner picked Espinosa's head up from the dirty ground, packing it away in a bag for the remainder of his trip to Pueblo. Once settled there, he boiled off the flesh and sold the murderous man's skull to one Professor Fowler, devoted phrenologist and collector of wanted men's heads. And thus Espinosa took his place in Professor Fowler's collection, one of many grinning criminals arrayed on a shelf in the good doctor's Denver office.

The legend would have us believe that Espinosa was not so happy to have his skull become a part of Fowler's medical collection. He began to appear in 1865, about two years after he was killed. Those early reports have him setting upon travelers in the twilight hours, a black, featureless silhouette of a rider atop a horse, looming over the trail anywhere along the Sangre de Cristo Pass. He always appeared sitting tall in the saddle with a rifle slung over his shoulder and, most notably, no head to speak of.

He would become Colorado's version of the Headless Horseman, haunting the passes of central Colorado in place of New York's Sleepy Hollow, wielding a Winchester instead of a sword. Also unlike Washington Irving's legendary phantom, Colorado's headless rider was bent on highway robbery.

There were some he didn't bother with. Soldiers making the trip to Fort Garland had little worth stealing, and the headless phantom was content to leave blue coats quaking in their boots, yet with their possessions intact. The reports began to spread after the end of the Civil War. Soldiers riding into Fort Garland in the evening whispered their experiences—the black, headless shadow mounted on a black horse with red eyes, descending upon the road with a shotgun in one hand and a machete in the other. Mounts as terrified as their riders bucked, reared and dashed away with their horrorstruck masters upon their backs. During the late 1860s, the arrival of such terrified retinues became an all too common occurrence in Fort Garland.

Others had more protracted experiences with the headless Mexican. Teamsters, settlers, prospectors and any other travelers who looked as though they may have something worth robbing often ran into Espinosa's spirit while traveling through the San Luis Valley and South Park. The interaction usually played out the same, with the headless phantom appearing at dusk and riding down before whatever frightened party, holding them at bay by the barrel of his gun while holding out his upturned palm in an unspoken demand—your money or your life. Few presented any quarrel to the black apparition, throwing down their possessions in wordless horror before galloping away.

Not everyone, however, was so easily cowed. Legend has one teamster named Charles Streeter confronting the spirit while riding late through the San Luis Valley. The story tells us he was heading south along the Sangre de Cristo road after completing a delivery to the mining camp of Placer. The early evening sky was between dark gray and deep purple when Espinosa's headless spirit suddenly appeared in the middle of the mountain road.

More angry than afraid at the sight of the figure on the road, Streeter pulled in his team, cursing aloud at the rider he had come so close to trampling. Cursing, that is, until he noticed that he was shouting at a black, headless silhouette that was pointing a shotgun at him with one hand and holding out the other. It took Streeter a few seconds to absorb the sight, and then he broke into a torrent of full-throated, open-mouthed, gap-toothed laugher. The archetypal westerner was brought up in a hard world whose material ambitions were as physical as the dangers he responded to. The sight of a headless gunmen, unable to see what it was shooting at, was nothing less than ludicrous to this hard-hearted man of the frontier.

"And what in tarnation do ye propose to do with that thing?" Streeter roared. "Ain't got no damn head to aim with!" With these words, Streeter put the leather to his team and headed on past Espinosa. "Just try and shoot me, ye useless fool!" he laughed as he went by. There was no shot fired, and when Streeter cast a glance back, the rider was no longer there.

Thanks to Streeter's love of drink and braggadocio, his encounter became the most-circulated account of Espinosa's spirit. Thus the tale of the headless Mexican lost some of its menace in the laughter. Nevertheless, Espinosa continued to haunt the road through South Park and the San Luis Valley, setting upon travelers who were not so able to laugh when confronted by the apparition. There is the account of Ramón Costa and Juan Sales, two ranch hands who were riding through the region in 1874. When the black rider leapt out onto the trail, the two young men were overcome by such frantic terror that they spurred their horses over the edge of a deep gulch to make their getaway. They were found the next day, both lying next to their dead mounts, limbs broken, shouting for help.

A short time later, Fort Garland's quartermaster, one Lieutenant Wilson T. Hartz, had a harrowing encounter with the phantom on his way from Placer to the fort. One look at the rider springing out of the trees, and Hartz was off down the trail at full speed. He galloped all the way to Garland, arriving at the fort in a state of near panic atop his frothing horse. His superior officer, at the gate when Hartz came streaking in, asked what the problem was. Looking into the stern eyes of the fort's commanding officer, the fear-stricken quartermaster made his best effort to calm down before issuing his clipped report: "Merely a small inconvenience upon the road."

And so the encounters with Espinosa's ghost continued. There were countless reports of run-ins with the mounted wraith through the rest of the century—always at dusk, always with those making their way through South Park or the San Luis Valley. Freighters, miners, campers, gentleman travelers: the apparition of the Mexican bandit did not discriminate, becoming more famous every time he appeared before terrified riders.

The most popular version of Espinosa's legend has him scouring the countryside in search of his missing head, in the belief that he would never find peace as long as his skull was an ornament in some doctor's office. This object of his tireless hunt was what he was demanding each time he held his open palm out to terrified travelers in the highlands of central Colorado.

Yet Espinosa's head was in a Denver office nowhere near the mountain roads he was haunting, a fact that did not deter him from continuing his futile search through much of the 20th century. There is reason to believe, however, that Espinosa has finally wised-up to this fact.

Traffic in the region is heavier than it has ever been, but decades have passed without a single sighting of the headless Mexican. It is true that a horseman would have an infinitely more difficult time robbing a motorized vehicle. Has the internal combustion engine convinced Espinosa that he has no choice but to move on to the great hereafter without his head? Perhaps. Or it could very well be that he still persists, only less visible now from within speeding cars, and not fast enough on his spectral steed to get motorists to stop. Whatever the case, the legend of Espinosa has worked its way out of travelers' nightmares and into the folklore of the region, one fanciful tale among many in the fanciful version of the state's history.

Belle Grant's Conversion

Redemption and reformation are major themes in the narratives of the world. There is the biblical conversion of Paul on the road to Damascus, or of Mary Magdalene after her seven demons were cast out. Shakespeare's Henry V renounces Falstaff and his dissolute ways upon taking up the mantle of king. And don't forget Goethe's Faust, who makes a pact with the devil but is saved in the end by virtue of his own quest for knowledge and experience. Even Wyatt Earp was said to have lost his way after his first wife, Urilla Sutherland, died of typhoid. He reeled through the next few years of life drunk and disorderly in the Indian Territory before pulling himself together to seriously school cowboys in Kansas and the Arizona Territory. The truth is, we as a people love tales of wayward souls who find their way. The characters who undergo these journeys from darkness into light resonate with so many others' perpetual need for rebirth and transformation.

Most people today do not know it, but Denver has its own, if much humbler, version of a "Paul on the road to Damascus" type of conversion. Her name was Belle Grant, and although her own epiphany did not lead to such historic consequences, it did save her life and contribute in its own modest way to the betterment of the city.

In the beginning, Belle was simply no good. In fact, Belle was flat out terrible. She arrived in Denver in the early 1880s on the arm of a devil of a sporting man whose name history has forgotten. Really, it does not matter what his name was, because the wild and corrupt Denver of those days was teeming with such men—men who lived by whiskey, women and the pursuit of easy money, however they could make it. Usually this meant sitting around card tables in smoky saloons, but exceptions could easily be made for murder, robbery and any other nefarious schemes that the more creative lowlifes were able to dream up.

Belle Grant was exceptional in that she was one of the few women in that debauched world who was as bad as, if not worse than, the men who ruled it. After a few days in Denver, she deemed the reprobate she had arrived with too mild for her vicious disposition and dumped him for a local tough who was rumored to be a murderer. It did not take her long to get bored with this man's company as well and gravitate to someone worse. Her affection usually lasted as long as it took for a richer murderer to walk into the room. And although she changed men as frequently as her boots, no man was permitted to break it off with her; she carried a derringer in her bodice and a knife in her boot just in case anyone was stupid enough to try. More than one man was said to have fled from Denver with one of Belle's bullets lodged in his anatomy. She passed five years in such a fashion, establishing a reputation as one of the young city's worst citizens.

For reasons unknown, in January of 1887 Belle was seized by the desire for a change of scenery. She telegraphed a friend named Lil, who was then enjoying the bedlam in Aspen, asking her if she would like to come along on a little sightseeing jaunt to Salt Lake City "to take a look and see," her message read, "if them Latter Day Saint boys got any sand in them."

So Lil came down to meet Belle, and the two women spent a few days raising a little Cain in Denver before getting on a westbound train to Utah. Like Paul on his way to Damascus, Belle underwent her conversion while she was on the road. The premonition hit her when they were stopped at a station along the way. It came to her through a voice, a woman's voice, familiar and chilling. It was as though an invisible presence was sitting right next to her, whispering a very specific message into her ear: she was to get off the train then and there; if she went any further west, her final ruin would surely follow.

Normally, Belle did not make a habit of listening to the advice of others, but this voice in her head spoke with a gravity she had never heard from the mouths of the living. It was hauntingly familiar, triggering a deep sadness from somewhere in her past, a needle in the muddled haystack of her memory. She looked at Lil, then, and told her friend that she needed to get off the train, if only to sleep one night before continuing on.

Lil was hardly on a strict schedule and got off the train with her friend, intent on finding the nearest saloon. When Belle informed Lil that she was in no mood for drink that night and was planning on getting to bed early, her friend raised an eyebrow but didn't say anything. All too aware of the loaded derringer Belle was surely packing in her bodice, she knew better than to start arguments with her fierce travel companion. Yet if she had looked closely enough, she would have seen that Belle's famous ferocity was already fading from her eyes.

A few hours later, Lil was off to see what kind of trouble she could make, and Belle was in her room alone, trying to ignore the fact that the invisible presence she had felt earlier on the train was still with her, somewhere in the room, perhaps standing in one of the darkened corners or on the chair. She could not say how she knew, but Belle also sensed that this presence was sternly examining her, and that it was not at all happy with what it saw. For the first time in years, Belle felt uncomfortably aware of herself—self-conscious of what she was doing with her life, and what she had done. She cast a quick glance at the mirror, not sure what to make of the stranger looking back at her. "Damned trains," she muttered, "never agreed with me—get me all funny in the head." With these words, the young woman laid back in bed, telling herself that all she needed was a little sleep. That was what she hoped, anyway, but the presence in the room had other plans.

"Belle! Belle!"

The young woman was up in a shot, derringer in hand, eyes darting frantically around the dark room. She looked at the bed next to her. Lil was not in yet. She was by herself. *But then who shouted my name?* She wanted to dismiss it as merely a dream, but knew in her gut this was not the case. The presence she had felt in the room before she had gone to sleep was still there. It was the first thing she was aware of when she flew up from her pillow.

And then, there it was—standing in the corner, still and silent, a black silhouette in the dark. She almost screamed. She aimed her pistol and almost fired. But something stopped her. The same authority she had heard in the voice that had spoken to her during the day was felt by her now, though she knew not who it belonged to. Nor why it was here. "Who are you?" Belle finally spoke, her quavering voice sounding strange to her own ears.

There was no response, and when she spoke, the figure in the corner seemed to fade, swallowed slowly by the darkness. *What the hell's going on in here?* she thought as she lay back down.

"Enough of your cursing, young lady. I'm sure I'm sick to death of your language after all these years." Belle sat up again. The voice was different than it had been. That day, it had come from *within*; she had heard it in her head. Now, however, she was hearing it with her ears. It was in the room.

"Who's there?" she said into the darkness. Her pistol was no longer in her hand, but she had her arm stretched forward. She had done this without thinking, driven by some instinct she did not understand—wanting, for some reason, to touch the voice that had just spoken.

"Close your eyes, and you'll see."

Belle did as she was told. She closed her eyes and the room was instantly flooded with light. Although her eyes were closed, she could see the room in front of her as though it was the middle of the day, with the sun flooding through the open windows. And there in the corner she saw the figure plainly. Her mother. Her long-dead mother just as she remembered her when she had been a girl. Her mother was young, her face stern and caring, in an austere dress that looked painfully starched around the buttoned-up collar. Belle was unable to move, unable to speak, unable to form a single clear thought.

"Hello, Belle," her mother said, moving slowly to where Belle was. When she was at the edge of the bed, she placed her palm on Belle's forehead and sat down next to her.

Belle thought, *Her hand is warm.* "Is that you, Mother?" she finally said. "But it's impossible. You died so many years ago." Tears formed in her eyes. The painful memories came flooding back. She had only been a girl when her mother died, left alone thereafter to fend for herself on the cruel frontier. She had almost forgotten what her mother looked like, how her voice sounded.

"I died, of course, but that doesn't mean I stopped watching over you," she said. "Do you really think you would still be alive if I hadn't been there? My Belle, with the life you live, you should have died 10 times over."

"But—" Belle began.

"No," her mother interrupted, "you don't owe your survival solely to your wits or your strength," she smiled. "Although I would not dream of belittling either."

"Mother—" Belle began again.

"Listen to me," her mother interrupted again. "I do not have very much time, and I can only say this once: you are in grave danger, Belle. This life you are living will be the death of you, and when the end comes, damnation awaits. My daughter, if judgment came today, you would most assuredly be cast into the fire." At this, the steel gaze of

Belle's mother softened. Lines appeared on her stern face. It was a subtle shift, but suddenly she looked on the verge of tears. "If that happens, I will never see you again, dear daughter. I ask you, I beg you: change your sinful ways. I do not want to think of an eternity without being able to see my beautiful daughter's face."

A single tear rolled down her mother's cheek, gathered at the edge of her jaw then fell onto Belle's hand, which was lying in her mother's lap. The moment the tear touched her hand, everything went black. Belle's room was dark again, and she was sitting on her bed with her eyes shut tight. When she opened them, she saw she was alone in her room. Not even a sense of the presence that had haunted her that day remained. The only indication that what had just transpired had actually happened was the teardrop that felt like ice against her knuckle.

"I swear, Mother," she said through her own freely flowing tears. "I swear I will change, from this day on."

Later on that morning, when Lil stumbled in from her night of carousing, Belle told her that she could continue on to Salt Lake City without her. She had some work to get started on back in Denver.

Lil looked at her, incredulous, and said, "What do you mean, *work*?"

The first thing Belle did upon returning to Denver was rent a small room as far away as she could get from the city's stretch of saloons and gambling houses. She began going to church every week, conscious of conducting herself, in manner and dress, with the utmost humility and respect. She volunteered her time to the local parish.

Instead of spending her nights getting drunk and seducing gamblers into giving her their dubious earnings, she spent her days knitting clothes for the poor and praying for the souls of the lost. When the Salvation Army set up in Denver, she was one of the first to join and became the organization's most tireless canvasser.

In short, Belle kept her word to her mother. When she died, many years later, a respected and well-loved woman, it was with a smile on her face and a certainty in her heart. She was going to see her mother again.

A Ghostly Accomplice

It was a sunny April morning in 1892, and Sheriff Deering of Gunnison County walked into his office whistling a tune he'd heard at the saloon the night before, telling himself that he was good and ready for another day at work. The sheriff's office, it should be said, was the Gunnison jailhouse. And it was currently occupied by three unsavory characters, none of whom were possessed of that charming, devil-may-care disposition that folklore often attributes to a good number of outlaws of the Old West.

Tom Burns was a burly murderer who killed a man in a dispute over a woman in Lake City, some 40 miles southwest of Gunnison. The cell next to him was occupied by a slippery eel of a man called Asktin, who had been arrested for forgery in the town of Creede. Topping off the distinguished trio was the scraggy prisoner in the third cell, long limbed and haggard beyond belief; he had stumbled into town a few days previous, mumbling to himself and leering at the local women. He was promptly arrested for no reason anyone could think of, besides the fact that he was obviously quite insane and creepy as anything.

"Rise and shine, sweethearts," Sheriff Deering called out as he walked into his office. "It's another day at the Hotel Gunnison—hope everyone slept well." The sheriff chuckled to himself, but was surprised at the silence that followed. His mockery was always followed by a quick, foul-tempered retort from Burns, who was usually eager to exhibit his particular dislike for the sheriff's sense of humor.

Deering took off his jacket and walked over to the door to the cellblock corridor. He peered through the bars, but his prisoners must have all been sitting against the back walls of their cells because none of them were visible. Loosening his revolver in its holster, the sheriff unlocked the door and walked into the corridor. He passed the lunatic's cell first—no surprises there. The man was curled up against the far wall of his cell, repeatedly running his bony hands over his neck and muttering to himself. "Hi there, acorn," Deering said, smiling and tipping his hat. The lunatic looked up at the sheriff and gnashed his teeth in response.

Next was Asktin who, of the three, the sheriff liked least. "Man's too clever for his own good," he often told his deputies. "That mouth of his is going to get him in more trouble than he's already in." The truth was that the sheriff fancied himself as quite the wit and could not bear the fact that, whatever he said, Asktin managed to one-up him. "Well, boy," he said to the con man, "you got anything for me today?"

On a normal day, Asktin would have several clever putdowns lined up for the sheriff. But on this morning, when the sheriff looked into the jail cell, he found himself facing quite a different man. Perspiring heavily and pacing back and forth across the back of his room, the quick-witted con did not even notice the sheriff. Deering called his name again.

"Oh!" the prisoner snapped out of his trance. "Hi there, sheriff," he said with a weak smile. The lawman could not help but notice that the usually grinning inmate looked wan and sweaty.

"I oughta have my head checked for asking this," Deering said, "but you okay, Asktin? You look like you've just seen your noose."

The prisoner nodded nervously and tried to smile. "Ain't nothing wrong with me a set of skeleton keys and a fast horse can't fix," he said. "Throw your mother in and you could call me king of Siam," he added.

"Glad to see you're coming around," Deering replied. He moved on to the last cell, where the homicidal Tom Burns was waiting. The sheriff was still approaching the cell of the dangerous man when he noticed something that made his heart jump. The cell door was unlocked. Somehow, the bolts had been pushed open; all it would take for Burns to be out in the corridor was a good shove against the door. *He plans on escapin'!* The sheriff's hand flew to his gun, and he pressed his back against the opposite wall of the corridor.

He had the hammer cocked back as he inched in front of Burns' cell. "I know what you're up to, Thomas Burns, you no-good mankiller!" the sheriff shouted, his words ringing in the narrow hall. "And I swear to God, I'll plug you full of holes without half a thought if you so much as think about goin' ahead with it!"

What Deering found when he lunged in front of the cell, however, was hardly a convict ready for action. Rather than being poised behind the door, Burns was lying on the floor, his face pressed against the smooth stone of the far wall. By the way his back was trembling, it looked as though he was weeping, but no sound escaped him.

The sheriff was in a momentary state of shock. Burns was one of the toughest, meanest scoundrels he had ever had the displeasure of watching over. The murderer had made it his habit to greet Deering with a hate-filled scowl and an ugly insult. He was condemned to the gallows, but the death sentence had done nothing to temper his ire. Now, there he lay, quietly sobbing into the wall.

"What the hell's wrong with you, Burns?!" the sheriff shouted. "And why is the bolt on your door thrown back?!" The visibly traumatized killer offered no response, and Deering took the opportunity to jump forward and refasten the bolts on the cell door. The sound of steel sliding against steel got Burns' attention. He stood up and turned to face Deering. His eyes were red and tear tracks cut lines down his grimy face before disappearing into his coarse black beard. His expression was a cross between extreme rage and total helplessness.

For Sheriff Deering, the sight conjured the thought of a schoolyard bully being put in his place, yet unsettled as he was by seeing Burns this way, Deering was not about to forget about the unlocked door. "The gallows finally getting to you, Burns? Well good, but you better tell me how the hell you got to these here bolts, and right quick!"

"I didn't touch 'em," Burns mumbled through his tears.

"Well then who did, the ghost of Jesse James?"

The sarcastic remark triggered something ugly in the convict. His face twisting in rage, he ran full tilt at the sheriff, crashing into the bars and causing the cell door to shudder with the impact. "D'you know anything about that abomination that just came through here, Deering, ye yellow good-fer-nothing?! You tell me, damn you! Did you know about it when you put me in here?!" His tears were running freely now, and he was pushing against the door with such force that Deering feared he was going to squeeze his face through the bars. The sheriff had no doubt that if he was able, Burns would not think twice about killing him. He had no words in the face of such hysterical rage and stood there mute, unable to respond.

Asktin's nervous laughter in the next cell was what snapped him out of it. "Don't mind Burns, sheriff," he said. "Man's just getting a tad nervous about having his neck stretched, is all."

"Asktin!" Burns roared. "You sniveling little worm! Don't tell me you didn't see it, too! Damn thing just walked out of here but 10 minutes ago!"

Asktin shrugged and gave the sheriff a meaningful look, circling his index finger around his ear. The lunatic in the far cell began to jabber: "Dead men with slit throats do not make fun cell mates. No they don't." This was the longest string of coherent words the madman had spoken since arriving in town.

The sheriff silenced them all. "Has this entire jailhouse gone loco!" he shouted. "Now I don't know what you think you're up to, Burns, but I'm not buyin' this crazy act for a minute. You unlocked this door schemin' on making an escape, and don't try'n tell me different!"

Burns managed to calm himself down somewhat. At least his face was no longer an enraged contortion, though his labored gasping still betrayed the fear in his heart. "Now, look, sheriff. You've got to get me out of this room. I don't care where you put me. Just get me out of here. No way I could make it through the night if it came back here. No way. I'm beggin' you."

Deering could only stand and stare. The Burns he knew had never asked for anything—now he was begging. "Show's over, Burns," he finally said. "Tell me straight, and tell me right now, how this door got unlocked."

"I'll tell you," the murderer breathed, "but only if you promise to get me out of here."

The sheriff laughed. "Sounds to me like you've forgotten a few things, Burns—something about you killing a man, one man at least. Something about me bein' a sheriff and this here bein' a jail. When was the last time you heard of a sheriff lettin' a killer he caught go free? Tell me, Burns, 'cause I'd like to know."

"Man's got a point," Asktin piped up from his cell.

"Put me in any cell but this one, I'm beggin' you. Or else just shoot me now. All I know is I'll do myself in if he comes back here."

"Who?!" shouted the sheriff.

"Truth is, I don't know who. But his skin was yellow and his damned eyes were dead. His throat was cut from one ear to the other, and his jacket was covered in blood that was long since dried."

The sheriff stared blankly, having no idea what to make of Burns' story. "That a fact?" he was finally able to manage.

"That's a fact," Burns continued. "He walked in here past midnight, calm and quiet like he was comin' home. I couldn't see clear at first, and I thought it was some fool from a lynch mob comin' after me, but then the moon poked out of them clouds and I got a better look. He was yellow and dead and covered in his own blood."

"You're telling me that this dead man, this…" Deering looked for the right word.

"Ghost, wraith, specter, spook, spirit from beyond," offered the con man in the next cell.

"Thank you, Asktin," the sheriff said, looking back to Burns. "This 'spirit from beyond' was what came in and unlocked this here door?"

"He stayed in here the whole night," Burns said. "Stood here an' looked at me all night, without sayin' a bleedin' word. Damn near drove me out of my mind. Then, when the sun was comin' up, he walked out slowly as he came. He put his hand through that door like it wasn't there and undid the bolt from the outside. Just like that."

"Now ain't that a special story," Asktin laughed. "A dead man comin' by to wish ol' Burnsy a how d'you do."

"Shut yer trap, fool!" Burns raged from the cell door. "You know damn well the thing happened. I heard you blubberin' like a baby last night. And don't say any differ-ent!"

Deering, Burns and Asktin stood there, soaking in the ramifications of the incredible story. The only sound in the jailhouse was the lunatic's muttering. He was saying the same thing, over and over: "They cut his throat 'cause he stole a horse."

Burns' story notwithstanding, Sheriff Deering knew for certain that there was no way Burns could have slid the bolts from inside his cell. Also, both the other cells were locked when he arrived, so Burns could not have been assisted by either of the others. But the sheriff was a practical man and did not believe the killer's story for a minute. Even if Burns had been visited by some kind of "spirit from beyond," as Asktin put it, why was the cell block door at the end of the corridor still locked when he arrived? All signs pointed to an attempted escape. He reasoned that somehow, Burns had managed to pull back the bolts on his cell door but wasn't able to get through the door at the end of the corridor.

Yet at the same time, he could not deny Burns' terror. Deering knew what a lying man looked like, and there was nothing in Burns' display that struck the lawman as false. And whatever else one wanted to say about the murderer in his cellblock, Burns was not the sort of man who found it easy to show any kind of weakness. Deering had been there when Burns had had his sentence read to him; he saw how the killer did not so much as flinch when he was told that he was going to meet his end on a hangman's noose. Now here he was, on the verge of blubbering.

"All right, I'll tell you what," the sheriff finally said, looking at the desperate killer before him. "Why don't I fix it so you and Asktin trade cells. How does that sound to you? But let me say this, if I come by tomorrow morning to find your cell door unlocked again, I'm going to shoot you on the spot. I'll do it, too; believe me, there isn't a single man I know who'd blame me for it."

Upon hearing the sheriff's resolution, Burns produced the widest grin Deering had ever seen on a condemned man. The killer looked so overjoyed that for a moment, the sheriff considered changing his mind. But then he saw the look on Asktin's face. The con man had been pale when Deering had entered, but now he looked like a "spirit from beyond" himself. "What's the matter, Asktin?" the sheriff grinned. "You don't look so talkative anymore."

It was Asktin's turn to break down. "Don't make me stay in there, sheriff," he said. "I don't know about no spirits from beyond business, but I'll vouch for Burns that something did walk into that cell last night. I saw it with my own eyes, and I reckon I don't want any part of it."

"Don't worry about it," Deering said. "If it's the devil you can take a few nights. Hell, you won't be seeing him again for a while yet. Burns has only got a few more days before he's going to be payin' him rent." Asktin did not find this funny in the least, and he broke out into blubbering protest when the sheriff got the two men to change cells by the barrel of his gun. And this was the way Deering left the three men in the jailhouse, giving his deputies orders to watch Burns' cell through the day in case he was working on another escape plan.

When Deering returned to the jailhouse the next morning, he was greeted with the same strange silence. "What's the matter?" he called into the cellblock. "You boys get another visit from Lucifer?" There was still no response, though he could hear a low whimpering coming from the cell at the end of the corridor, where Asktin was now imprisoned. He unlocked the cellblock door and walked past the lunatic, who looked up at him and gnashed his teeth, past Burns' cell, where the killer was flat on the floor with his back to the door, and on to Asktin's cell, where, sure enough, the bolt was unlatched, and Asktin was a complete mess.

The con man was not nearly as composed as the killer had been. As soon as he saw Sheriff Deering standing in the hall, he let out a grateful cry and rushed out into the corridor, falling at the lawman's feet and kissing his boots. "I'll do whatever it takes. All the money I conned off those old ladies is buried a few miles out of town. I'll take you there if you let me go. We can give it back to 'em. We can keep it for ourselves: 50-50. Hell, you can have it all. Just please, sheriff, don't make me stay in that cursed cell another night."

"Let me guess," the sheriff said. "You got a visit in the middle of the night. He's the one who unlocked your door. Am I right?"

"I've got no idea about the unlocked door," Asktin blubbered. "And I don't care, just don't make me stay in there another night. Like I said, I'll do anything."

Having seen Burns lose his composure already, the sheriff was not as surprised by this prisoner's hysterics. "You're a smart man, Asktin," he said to the man sobbing at his feet. "Maybe you can answer me this question."

The con nodded his eager assent.

"Lets say, just for a minute, there's some truth to these stories of how the devil, a spirit from beyond, or what have you, is visiting my jailhouse at night. Now, why is it that when this man—or thing, or whatever it is—why is that he unlocks the cell door here when he leaves, but keeps the cellblock door all shut up? Let's face it, he isn't going to get out without unlocking that door, so why does he bother shutting it behind him when he goes? If there's this bleeding guy, ghost, whatever, breaking into my jailhouse in the middle of the night just to spend time with the likes of you, why wouldn't he have the common courtesy to leave the door unlocked so you'd be able to make your getaway?"

When the response came, it was not from Asktin, but from the madman down the hall. "Because," the voice rasped, "the fools did not *ask*."

"Well look here!" exclaimed the sheriff. "Sounds like someone's got something to say." He strode over to the first cell in the hall, where the lunatic was confined. "So tell me, my friend, are you of the opinion that you would be able to convince this visitor to bust you out of here?"

The lunatic sprung up to his haunches and shot a yellow grin at the sheriff. "Why would I want to do that?" he hissed. "I feel no need to escape. I am enjoying it fine here."

"But you're telling me you would be able to speak to him?" the sheriff asked.

"Bah! I've spoken to him many times," the lunatic said. "Sometimes he wanders in the mountains."

"So you're old friends then," the sheriff said.

"No. I have no friends. But I know him. They slit his throat for stealing a horse."

"I suppose you wouldn't mind, then, if you spent the night in his cell," Deering said, "seeing as how you're already acquaintances."

The madman shrugged. "I have no problem sharing space with the dead. These mountains are full of them."

Sheriff Deering looked down the hall to where Asktin was still lying prostrate on the ground. "You hear that, Asktin? You're in luck; this good gentleman's volunteered to take your cell."

As cavalier as he seemed about the situation, Deering took precautions that day. Before nightfall, he and his men examined every inch of the cell in question, looking for any possible tools that prisoners were using to pry open the cell door. He also added a number of locks to the existing bolt system. Whatever happened, Sheriff Deering did not want to turn up the next morning and discover that the madman was able to slip past that cell door.

He arrived the next day to a sight that was infinitely worse. The sheriff's heart began pounding the moment he spied the jailhouse from down the street; the front door of the jailhouse was wide open, swinging on its hinges in the early morning breeze. Pulling his revolver, he set spurs to his horse. Without so much as a pause, Deering raced into the jailhouse, already knowing in his gut what he was going to see.

Sure enough, the cellblock door was wide open, and he could see before he reached the threshold that the three cell doors in the corridor were open as well. He resigned himself to the fact then and there: they were gone, without a doubt. Somehow, he had missed something. They must have been working together. There was a plan, some trick, which he had played right into. Surely.

He checked the first cell, where Asktin had been interred the night before. Empty. He moved on to the second cell, the ramifications of its wide open door far more serious than the first. Tom Burns, a convicted killer, was at large in Gunnison county. And he had gotten away on *his* watch. He began to turn, not wanting to waste any time getting together a posse to hunt down the two escaped criminals. The escaped lunatic in the last cell did not concern him. There was a killer on the loose. But he had not taken his first step when a terrible, lingering chuckle made him stop. It was coming from the third cell, where the prisoners insisted they had encountered their otherworldly visitor.

His blood froze. Up until this moment, he had not allowed himself to even consider the possibility that there was anything to the men's stories—but what was that laugh? With goose bumps tickling his arms and neck, Deering crept forward. At the door, he exhaled once, steadied his gun hand, and leapt into the doorway, ready to shoot. His jaw dropped. It was not a pale specter with a slit throat. It was the lunatic. He was rocking back and forth on his haunches, a ghastly smile twisted across his face.

"What are you doing here?" Deering quavered.

"I told you, I have no interest in leaving."

"What happened? How did they get away?" the sheriff pressed.

"Do you really need to be told again? The visitor. He came by. We spoke. Not the most pleasant man, really, but how can you blame him, walking around with a slit throat."

The sheriff cupped his face in his hands, shaking his head in confusion. "But he did not unlock the cellblock door before. He never let them out before."

"That was because no one asked," the lunatic said, and threw his head back to produce a shrieking, maniacal laugh.

This laugh echoed in Deering's mind as he ran of the jailhouse that morning. It was still there when he rode out at the head of his posse in search of the two criminals. And it would remain there for his entire life, whenever he thought about what transpired in his jailhouse those three fateful nights in 1892. Burns and Asktin were never found. The lunatic vanished from his cell a few days after the escape.

The House in Coyote Gulch

The Jameson brothers had noticed the dark clouds looming early that morning but had hitched the wagon to the
horses anyway, hoping that the weather would not turn
as bad as it looked. The ride to Franktown from their
Douglas County farm was a half-day's ride at least, and
they were sure they were going to get some rain, but their
father insisted they make the trip. Their plow was in
urgent need of repair, and the tools were in town. "It better be rainin' something fierce if I don't see you boys back
today," he had warned them before they left.

That was a good nine hours ago, and Matthew and
John were still holed up. They lucked upon an abandoned
ranch house early that afternoon, when the storm picked
up from bad to plain crazy. The rain was pounding on the
house like a hundred thousand hammers falling from the
sky. The thunder was seconds behind the lightning, and it
had been that way for well over an hour now. "It ain't getting any further away," young John said, referring to the
thunder that had just boomed and echoed through the
darkening sky.

"Maybe it likes it here," said the elder Matthew, his
nose buried in a can of beans they had brought along.
The brothers had resigned themselves to the fact that they
were going to be spending the night in the deserted ranch
house. The storm was showing no sign of letting up, and
besides, it was getting too dark for safe travel, especially
considering how muddy the trail was sure to be.

The idea did not bother Matthew so much. Difficult as their father could be, there was no way he would blame them for not making the full trip back in this weather. And as for spending the night in a deserted old ranch house—dirty, leaking and strewn with the long-abandoned belongings of some other family—Matthew barely gave it a thought. As tough and practical as his father was, Matthew just did not have it in him to get spooked by their undeniably creepy surroundings.

John, however, was having a much more difficult time with it. Something about the place bothered him deeply. There was the sound the wind made as it blew through the gaps in the wood planks, a sound partway between a moan and a scream, depending on how hard it was gusting. The rain leaked through the sagging ceiling and decrepit walls, leaving dark stains on the wallpaper that still hung here and there in patches. The fire they had lit in the hearth did not make things any more inviting. It only made the scene that much more forlorn, casting shivery light on the dirt and discarded effects of whoever had once called the place home. Two buffalo horns were still mounted over the doorway to what had once been the kitchen, and there were a few empty bottles in the corner of the room they sat in. They had been using the decayed furniture for firewood.

"Who do you think lived here?" John asked, needing to break the silence.

Matthew did not look up from his beans. "Ranchers, I reckon."

"Don't it give you the shivers none?" was John's next question.

Matthew finally looked up, a grin spreading across his bristly young face. "Awwww, look at that, will ya? Little Johnny's scared of the ghosts in the spooky old house. Ya want I should ride out and get Ma for ya?"

John snorted his contempt and pretended to look nonchalant. "Didn't say I was scared. Just wonderin' if *you* were, fool. I ain't yellow. Ain't scared of nothing."

Matthew went back to his beans. "Sure, John," he smiled, "I know you ain't."

But he spoke too soon. For at that moment, the sky outside lit up with a brilliant blue flash, followed almost instantly by a splitting peal of thunder—and then came the scream. It was the most terrifying sound either one of them had ever heard. High-pitched and agonized, it reached octaves of pain and terror neither brother had the capacity to imagine. And it sounded from within the house they were holed up in, upstairs, where neither had been yet.

John let out an involuntary shout and grabbed his brother, who was looking up at the ceiling with no small measure of alarm in his normally stoic eyes. A minute passed in dreadful silence before John gathered the courage to speak. "What in all abomination was that?" he hissed over the sound of the rain.

"It was Pa," the elder brother finally snorted. "He's mad as a banshee that we didn't make it back in time."

"Nothing to joke about, Matty. I'm thinking there's somebody up there."

"Doubt it, but I'm going to take a gander regardless." A spark of terror flashed through John's eyes at the suggestion, and he grabbed Matthew's pant leg when his elder brother stood up. "What are you doing?" he snapped at his younger brother. Then he softened his tone, seeing how terrified John was. "Don't worry about it, John. I'm just taking a quick look, just in case somebody up there needs help."

"That's not it, Matty. I swear. There's something *unnatural* about this place. I can *feel* it. We've got to get out of here. And quick."

Matthew was careful to maintain a calm demeanor. "What, into that?" he gestured to the storm outside. "You gone loco, man? There's no traveling in that storm."

"But what if there's some kind of maniac up there? Some kind of murdering hermit who's just waiting?"

"Hell, if that's the case, then I better go up there before he comes down here," Matthew reasoned.

John shot a glance around the abandoned room and felt a new wave of panic welling up. "Don't leave me down here, Matty! Please, brother! Don't go up there. Let's just pretend nothing happened. Let's stay down here 'til daybreak."

"Don't be daft, John." There was a trace of irritation working its way into the elder brother's voice. "What would Dad say about this—you blubbering like a baby? Stay put. I'll be back down in a minute." With these words, Matthew turned his back on his terrified brother and mounted the narrow staircase.

John clutched his knees to his chest as the stairs groaned under his brother's weight. There was the sound of his footsteps above, and dust showered down from the ceiling. It was obvious his brother was walking slowly, choosing his steps carefully, no doubt, on the sagging floor. Then, there was silence. The rain continued to fall, the wind continued to blow, the thunder continued to roll. Long minutes passed without so much as a sound from above. John's fear mounted. His blood went cold. The shadows came to life. He prodded at the fire. When he broke the swelling silence, it was at the top of his voice. "Matty! What the hell you doing up there?"

His brother didn't respond. "I said Matty! Quit your fooling and get your behind back down here. I'm not kidding around, man!" When several more minutes passed without a reply, John lost his composure and broke down, bawling openly, tears streaming down his cheeks.

He shouted his brother's name again. And when there was still no answer, he broke a leg off a chair, wrapped one end with a rag, jabbed it into the fire and proceeded up the stairs, the makeshift torch in his shaking hand. At the top of the stairs was a short, narrow hall that ended at an open doorway. Beyond was a single garret room under an angled ceiling. By the flickering light of his torch, he saw a filthy curtain twisted before the room's single window, which was open to the storm beyond. Broken glass littered the floor underneath it, and the warped night table next to it was on the verge of collapse. There was also a rusted bed frame and a rotting mattress covered in leaves, garbage and rodent droppings. But his brother was nowhere to be found. "Matty?" John whispered into the room, refusing to believe his eyes. "Matty, where the hell are you?"

John crept into the room, navigating the soft floor-boards with care. He slowly passed the bed and the night table. At the window, he brushed the billowing curtain aside and looked out. Lightning flashed and he saw the landscape clearly for an instant—the ravine they were nestled in, the thick stands of trees. There below were the horses. It seemed like an eternity ago, now, when they rode down into the gulch seeking shelter from the storm.

The memory of that frantic ride triggered a thought in John's mind, and it was a thought that paralyzed him. *The gulch!* He had thought of it when they were riding down earlier that day, but had quickly forgotten under the fury of the storm. They were riding into Coyote Gulch. He had recalled, for a moment, the childhood stories he and his friends told one another at school about Coyote Gulch and the old abandoned McIntyre House. That was where they were. Everyone knew the McIntyre House was possessed.

The thought came and he felt a cold well within. There was a voice inside telling him to turn around. Lightning flashed, thunder rumbled and there, not five feet from where he was standing, was a man he had never seen before. In the next instant, another terrible shriek filled the room—the same sound as before, except louder now, coming from inside the room, right next to him.

John jumped and hollered. He saw the figure in the room flash out of sight and then he ran, tearing out of the bedroom and practically tumbling down the stairs. He had no idea what had happened to Matthew. In those frantic moments as he threw together his belongings, put on his hat and jacket and threw open the door, he was convinced that his brother was gone, claimed somehow by the ghosts of the evil McIntyres, who surely still resided in their infamous home.

Just as he flung open the door a man stumbled over the threshold, and John screamed as he backpedaled, his fists raised. It took him a few confused seconds to register the man's laughter. "Did you just *scream*, Johnny?" It was Matthew.

John did not hesitate for a second, unabashedly throwing his arms around his brother, grabbing his arms and shoulders to make sure he was real. "You're here! You're here!" he shouted.

"Well, where the hell else would I be?" Matthew replied, pushing his brother off him. "What's gotten into you?"

"What the hell's gotten into you?" John shot back. "Disappearing like that in this godforsaken place on this godforsaken night."

"Look, I went up there into that bedroom and swore I saw a guy jumping out the window," Matthew said. "I only saw him for a second, but it looked like he needed help, so I followed him out."

John was holding his breath. "Well? Did you find him? What was wrong with him?"

"There's no one out there. I looked all around and couldn't see him anywhere," Matthew replied with a shake of his head. "There's no way anyone could have moved that fast. I was right behind him."

"Because he wasn't there! There was no one there!" John's eyes were wide as he shouted out his revelation. "This is the McIntyre House, Matty! It's full of ghosts!"

"The McIntyre House," Matthew said more to himself than his younger brother. He had not even thought about it. It had been years since he attended the spelling and arithmetic lessons at the schoolhouse. The stories about the McIntyre House came back all at once, and he stared at the interior of the house in wonder, consciously suppressing a physical shudder. "We must be the biggest fools in the county," the young man breathed. "Get your stuff together, Johnny; we're getting out of here pronto!"

But John already had his belongings with him; he watched his brother quickly gather his own things before both ran out into the rain to ready the wagon. With a whip and a shout, the Jameson brothers drove their horses out of Coyote Gulch, happily risking the storm over a night in the McIntyre House. On the way out, John told Matthew what had happened in the second floor bedroom, and the elder brother, though just as tough and practical as his father, did not doubt a word.

As a rule, folks in the country south of Denver stayed away from the McIntyre House. McIntyre and his two boys had built the house tucked into Coyote Gulch in 1871; that part of the gulch became a place to avoid soon after. The clan just had bad news written all over them—it was as simple as that. The senior McIntyre had a boorish manner and an acid mouth that put the meanest cowpunchers to shame, and his wife, a poor, downtrodden woman, walked with the air of someone who knew fear as a constant companion.

But as detestable as Mr. McIntyre was, he was nowhere near as bad as the two sons from his first marriage, Jack and Jim. Practically indistinguishable from one another, these two spitting, snorting specimens belonged to the bottom rung of frontier society. They were violent parasites who subsisted by stealing from the men around them, but their little rustling operation down in the gulch was nothing grand. The trio lacked the ambition and imagination for large-scale crime. They were content to do just enough to get by. They sneaked out at night into neighboring ranchers' herds and rustled the first livestock they came across.

No one liked the McIntyres, which was fine, because they did not like anyone else. Their end of Coyote Gulch became a place that locals stayed clear of, but no one told the hapless man traveling through by stage from Denver to Pueblo in June 1873. Unfortunately, his ride left without him after a rest stop at the Twenty Mile House station. Nursing no small amount of frustration, the man decided to walk to the next stop at Russellville, 10 miles away, where, if no other stage came by that day, there was a hotel he would be able to lodge in for the night.

On that day, fate would intercede in the cruelest imaginable way. A heavy thunderstorm broke while the man was on the road. He ran into Coyote Gulch to take shelter and saw the lights of the McIntyre House shining among the trees. Having heard nothing of the family's reputation, he did not hesitate to approach. The senior McIntyre answered the door scowling, but the frown quickly dissolved when the soaking wet traveler informed him of his quandary. Here, the old man thought, was an opportunity not to miss.

It is impossible to know how far old McIntyre was willing to take the situation. It would not matter, however, for his dissolute sons, Jack and Jim, took over for their father as soon as they staggered over to see who was knocking in the middle of such a storm. Taking stock of the lost traveler standing out in the rain, all three McIntyre men found themselves thinking the same thing. Yes. Here, most definitely, was an opportunity.

They welcomed the man in with wide grins. They fed him the best cut of meat from one of their stolen animals. They opened up their best bottle of whiskey and regaled him with stories of ranching adventures late into the night. When the man grew too weary to keep his eyes open, they offered him the best bed in the room upstairs. Old man McIntyre and his wife would sleep down in the main room that night. The man did not want to accept such an offer, but they insisted, and so he went on upstairs, amazed at the hospitality of this humble frontier family.

He never made it through the night. No one can say exactly what the three McIntyre men discussed in hushed voices after their guest fell asleep. It is impossible to know how the decision was reached—who suggested it, if there was any disagreement, how it would be carried out. But what matters is that the decision was made; sometime past midnight, the McIntyres were resolved. There was going to be a murder.

So as to avoid waking the man by walking up the creaking staircase, Jack and Jim climbed into the bedroom through the window. The traveler was asleep when one of the brothers sunk a knife into the man's chest. Yet until this night, the McIntyres were cattle rustlers, not murderers, and they did not know anything about killing humans. The blade was mishandled, and the man woke from his sleep screaming in agony and terror, the knife protruding from his chest.

He leapt to his feet and the two McIntyre brothers were immediately on him, one jabbing the knife deeper, the other trying to knock him back onto the bed. But the man kept them both at bay until Jack drew another knife and stabbed the man again. The second wound was the one that did it, and the traveler collapsed, breathing his last on the bedroom floor.

Jack and Jim did not waste any time. As they discovered that night, murder and robbery came quite naturally to them. They rifled through the dead man's belongings, taking his gold, his watch, his wallet, even stripping him of his boots and hat before hauling his body out the window. They buried him that night in the pouring rain, out among a stand of trees.

The crime, however, did not go unpunished. When word got out that a traveler out of Denver had disappeared somewhere between Twenty Mile House and Russellville, all eyes turned to Coyote Gulch. A posse of armed men rode down on the McIntyre House a few days later. Storming into the home, the posse quickly found the bloodstains on the bed, all over the floor and on the windowsill. It was all the evidence they needed. No one liked the McIntyres to begin with, and a nearby tree was promptly outfitted with three nooses. And yet to the chagrin of many men in the posse, only one of those ropes would be used that day.

During the course of the impromptu investigation, young Jack McIntyre managed to make his getaway, disappearing into the trees of Coyote Gulch, and then from the Colorado Territory altogether. As for the senior McIntyre, he was saved thanks to Mrs. McIntyre's pleas and Jim's insistence that his father had nothing at all to do with the crime. Thus Jim alone went to the makeshift gallows to be hanged while his father and stepmother looked on. He was buried without ceremony at the base of that tree.

As the reader already knows, the story does not end here. The McIntyres promptly left the territory, and as soon as word of the incident got out, Coyote Gulch became widely regarded as cursed. It was damned forever by the brutal crime that was committed there and by the spirit of the lonely traveler, who for many years afterward was still heard screaming for his life on stormy summer nights.

Guilty Without Trial

Sometime past midnight, on December 15, 1877, Robert Schamle, half-starved and barefoot, was led out into the snow-covered streets of Georgetown. A noose hung around his neck, and the six masked men around him were spitting their taunts, jabbing him with their pistols and yanking hard at the noose. There was laughter when he collapsed into the snow. "That's the way! Give 'im a little taste of what he's in for!" One of the men kicked him in the gut before he was hauled back up.

Robert Schamle was well aware that he was going to die that night. The "Our Father" was spilling from his lips in his native German, the automatic cadence of his prayer uninterrupted by the harsh laughter and catcalls of the six burly men. When Albert Selak's barn came into sight, he began to fight. One of his tormenters received a sudden fist in the face; another, an elbow to the throat. For a few seconds he was free, and he ran as fast as his shaking legs could take him. But when he slipped in the snow, the men were on him before he even hit the ground. He was soundly thrashed for trying to escape, and they hauled him up again.

The horrible stench of Colonel Selak's pigpen reached them, as well as the squeals and snorts of the beasts within. "Ye smell that, boy?!" one of the men hollered. "That's where it all ends!" He looked close into Schamle's terrified eyes and rapped the man's head with a closed fist. "Ye understand? Did ye get that?" He jabbed his thumb at the barn, enunciating every syllable. "That's where you're gonna die!"

They dragged him inside, threw a rope across one of the rafters and tied the end to the noose around his neck. "Now we're gonna pull you up and see what happens, all right?" one of the men said, clapping him on the shoulder.

"Tell us if it hurts," one of the others added.

With those words, two men yanked on one end of the rope, hoisting their prisoner up by his neck until his dangling legs were twitching in the air. They tied the rope to a beam, then, and sat back and watched as Schamle was slowly strangled. The last sounds the dying man heard were the laughter of the men and the squealing of the pigs shuffling underneath.

Robert Schamle died at 32 years of age. He was an Austrian immigrant completely alone in the great wide expanse of frontier America. In a time and a place where everyone was an outsider of sorts, Schamle, thin, gawky and barely able to speak the language, stood out for his exceptionally outlandish air, especially in the settlement of Georgetown.

Georgetown had something of an unusual reputation among the other western towns at the time. Its nickname was the "Silver Queen," coined by the many Victorian British who came to the area seeking a taste of the much-talked-about boomtown experience on the American frontier. These were not typical British citizens either, but young adventurers from the upper classes, restless scions of some of the best families in the Empire. Perhaps it could be called the Aspen of its day, filled with wealthy visitors looking to enjoy the great outdoors.

Schamle could not have found a less hospitable place to make his home. Arriving in August 1877, just four months before he was so brutally murdered, Schamle was almost instantly relegated to the lowest caste—it was inevitable after one look at his shabby dress, his ungainly manners and his barely functional grip on the English language.

Nevertheless, Schamle seemed determined to make a life there, getting work as an assistant butcher at G. Edward Kettle's slaughterhouse. His boss was a man named Henry Theide, a German butcher of considerable girth whose diet was most definitely influenced by his trade. Theide, married with three children, was popular among the men of the town for his jovial if somewhat coarse disposition, known equally for his temper and his generosity. He offered the broke and homeless Schamle a room in his home soon after they began working together, at least until the new immigrant was able to get on his own two feet.

While he was working for solvency, the Austrian was having a hard time finding his place in this terribly class-conscious little town. In the saloons and billiard club that he frequented, he was constantly being judged on his rough appearance and less-than-charming demeanor. So, in an effort to fall in with some of the haughty townsfolk, he began making up stories of being descended from gentry in one of the middle European countries—sometimes Germany, other times Switzerland. No one took him very seriously, however. Imagine, the descendent of Swiss wealth holed up in a room in Henry Theide's home, bloodying his hands daily by cutting meat. His lies were so outrageous that the harder Schamle tried to fit in, the more scorned he became.

His claims that he belonged to the upper classes were even less convincing when it became obvious how hard and reliable a worker he was. Always at the butcher shop when he was supposed to be, Schamle turned out to be the best workmate Theide ever had. Schamle knew very little about the butcher's trade when he arrived, but he improved quickly under Theide's tutelage. He was soon nearly as competent with the knife as the brawny German.

It is impossible to say how far he would have gone with his newfound profession, for on October 14 of that year, everything changed. That Sunday morning, Henry Theide was found lying on the slaughterhouse floor, his butcher's apron stained with his own blood, a gaping bullet hole in his chest. There was an uncut side of beef on the chopping block, and his butcher knife lay just beyond his lifeless grasp. And Robert Schamle was nowhere to be found.

Almost instantly, the Austrian was assumed to be guilty. Word spread about how Theide had had $90 on his person on Saturday, yet there was no money on him when he was found dead the next day. As well, one of Schamle's drinking acquaintances, a man named Matt Parsons, told everyone he knew that Schamle had borrowed a pistol from him on the 12th. Schamle had told Parsons that he wanted the pistol to shoot chickens at the slaughterhouse because the one thing he hated about his job was taking the cleaver to the still-living creatures.

It was settled, then. Not only was he missing, but he was also in possession of the weapon, and the missing $90 was considered motivation enough for the poverty-stricken Austrian. Residents of Georgetown found it easy to vilify Schamle. It went beyond the deed he was accused of. The zeal with which the local papers attacked him revealed an undeniable eagerness to brand the outsider. And why not? He had always appeared not quite right in the community's eyes, what with his long, skinny arms and legs, his awkward gait, his vacant stare and his terrible English. And there were all those ridiculous stories he told about being descended from Old World bourgeois. He was obviously guilty of the cold-blooded and calculated murder—$90 for a man's life.

When the editorial sections of the *Courier, Miner* and *Silver Standard* were done with him, Schamle was pure evil lurching through Clear Creek County, a rabid murderer who would just as soon shoot a man as greet him. The bigger papers in Denver picked up the story and ran with it, and it was not long before Schamle's likeness was stamped all over the region, along with the caption, "Wanted: Dead or Alive"—preferably the former. The few voices that clamored for a man's right to a fair trial—that even in these circumstances, a man was innocent until proven guilty—were shouted down by the masses.

Schamle did not have a good grasp of English, but he knew enough to gather that he was in trouble. But if there is any truth to eyewitness accounts, he did not seem to recognize *how much* trouble he was in, which seemed to suggest his possible innocence during the investigation. In the first few places he stopped in the days after Theide's body was found, Schamle found odd jobs for food and a bed. He did not use a pseudonym. Furthermore, the families that gave him work spoke of his obvious need. Haggard and hungry as he looked, he always worked hard for whatever food was provided him. No one who encountered him claimed to feel threatened in any way. The obvious question arose: if Schamle had made off with the dead butcher's $90, why would he make such a plodding exit from Georgetown, taking day-long stops here and there to earn enough food to continue? With $90, a man could make a fast getaway to the farthest reaches of the territory and effectively vanish without a trace.

But at the very end of the manhunt, Schamle had indeed been using an assumed name. If he was innocent, why would he later take on an alias? Could plain stupidity account for it? A captured Schamle would later insist that he only changed his name when he discovered that Theide was dead. He claimed that he and Theide had gotten into a quarrel about the proper method for cutting a side of beef. Taken aback that the usually meek Schamle was telling him how to do his job, Theide had lost his considerable temper and had come at his assistant with his butcher knife. Schamle knew full well that he would never be able to wrestle the knife from the much bigger man, so he turned and ran. As he went, he grabbed Matt Parsons' pistol off the table and fired blindly behind him, hoping, in his terror, that this would deter Theide from following. He insisted that he did not know he had shot the butcher, and that he definitely did not rob him. He claimed to know nothing about the $90.

If there was any truth to this story, if Schamle did indeed shoot Theide in self-defense, then the law dictated considerable clemency in his sentencing. Yet such arguments were meaningless to the enraged people of Georgetown. Captured in mid-December in a boardinghouse in West Las Animas, Schamle went into custody peacefully. From there, the law transported him to Pueblo and then finally, under the custody of the sheriff of Clear Creek County, back to Georgetown. An angry mob waited there at the train station, and the bewildered Austrian came under a barrage of insults, stones and rotten fruit. Imprisoned in the Georgetown jailhouse, he was abducted and murdered a few days later.

Robert Schamle's death was greeted with a general elation. For most of the next day, his body was left to hang in Albert Selak's pigpen, where it was visited by nearly everyone in Georgetown. It seemed that only Selak, who was less than pleased that there was a body hanging in his barn, hesitated at joining the party.

Everyone knew that the approving Sheriff Easley would forgo a formal investigation. Even while Shamle's body still hung in the barn, the jailhouse was raided for his belongings. An impromptu auction was held for the accused killer's boots, hat and whatever other meager possessions he owned. The man who bought his hat got it for 5 cents, and the boots went to another for 50 cents.

His body was cut down soon after that. It was said that his head struck a barrel as he was carried off, leaving a dark trail of blood on the lid from the head wounds he had suffered the night before. He was thrown into a burlap sack and buried without ceremony in an unmarked grave at the edge of town. And so passed Robert Schamle—or so Georgetown residents thought.

The uneasiness began roughly a week after he was buried, when the man who had purchased Schamle's boots was found dead in Denver; he had apparently taken his own life. Around the same time, Albert Selak decided to burn the barrel that had been smeared with Schamle's blood. Every day the stain seemed to get darker, and no matter how hard he tried, it would not wash off. He finally took the barrel out and lit it on fire. Within a week, half of his pigs had contracted some sort of strange disease and gone mad, attacking one another and crashing against the pen walls, lunging at anyone who came too close. Selak was forced to kill every pig that had fallen ill.

Out on the edge of town, strange noises were heard coming from the mound where Schamle was buried. The frigid winter winds carried the eerie wails through Georgetown, setting everyone on edge. Some attributed the strange sound to wild animals and pranksters, but there was not a soul who heard these noises and did not think of the man who had been hanging in Selak's barn.

According to legend, Schamle began appearing before townsfolk right around Christmas that year. The sighting in the town jail was the one that got everyone talking. John Saunders, the man who had been guarding Schamle the night he was lynched, was asleep at his post. It was coming up on Christmas, after all, and it was a suitably slow night in the caboose, with only one reveler sleeping off a charge of public drunkenness. The wind was howling and the snow was falling heavily, but all was well for Saunders, lying tucked beside a roaring hearth, fast asleep. That was until the jailer was woken by a cold blast of wind that tore through the jail. He snapped from his sleep, thinking that someone had come in. In a sense, someone had, though Saunders refused to believe his eyes. There, looking as real as anyone else, was Robert Schamle, standing barefoot and ragged, exactly as he had appeared during his last night on earth, staring at him blankly. Saunders shouted and turned to reach for his lantern, but by the time he had it lit, the apparition had vanished.

He waited for his heart to slow, took a few deep breaths and told himself the only thing he could—that it had been a bad dream. The next morning, however, he woke to find a set of footprints in the freshly fallen snow that led out of the jailhouse. They were odd for two reasons: first, no one had been in the jailhouse all morning; and second, the footsteps came to a mysteriously abrupt stop in the snow after a few yards—there was no indication whatsoever of where the person who had made them went from there. Saunders quickly spread the news, and the return of Robert Schamle was soon on everyone's lips.

Saunders was not the only person who claimed to see a ghostly manifestation of the murdered Austrian. Back at the Selak barn, Albert's son was feeding the pigs one day when he was seized by the notion that he was not

alone. He heard a loud wail from the corner of the pig-
sty. Looking over, he saw a gaunt, barefoot man huddled
there. Dropping the bucket of feed, he ran to his father
and dragged him back. There was no sign of Schamle
when they returned, but Albert never made his son feed
the pigs again.

These were just some of the phenomena that were said
to occur in and around Georgetown that winter. Elizabeth
Selak, Albert's wife, claimed to have seen a shadow hanging from a phantom noose once as she walked by the
barn. After Christmas, Saunders was woken a few more
times by the same apparition, though the tracks in the
snow never repeated themselves. Countless sightings of
an emaciated young man were reported around town,
appearing one moment, gone the next.

There has been a fair amount of speculation, since
Schamle's lynching and concurrent haunting, that the
Austrian may well have been telling the truth. It is entirely
possible that he shot Theide in fear, to ward off an attack.
The butcher's own wife would later go on the record to
say that such behavior was not at all atypical of her former husband, who could fly into terrifying fits if pro-
voked. Could Schamle, then, have been killed mainly
for looking different? For not fitting in? If so, this would
explain the restless spirit that haunted this once terribly
selective frontier town.

2
Restless Miners

The Mamie R. Mine

Compared to the feverish enthusiasm of most gold rushes in the American West, the gold mining in Colorado's Cripple Creek region had surprisingly tentative, if not downright skeptical, origins. Located in central Colorado, 25 miles west of Pikes Peak, the Cripple Creek area was a quiet place, used by local homesteaders mostly for grazing livestock. One would think that Bob Womack's discovery of gold in 1874 would have made the quiet creek into another one of the West's gold-digging Gomorrahs, but no such thing happened…well, not *yet* anyway.

Spurred on by his modest 1874 finding, Womack put his back into the job. He must have been imbued with an amazing stubbornness, because 16 years passed before he made another strike—16 years of working alone, obstinately boring into the ground while the other gold diggers rushed from one bonanza to another. He was unmoved when they announced that there was gold in the Black Hills in 1876; he barely even looked up when word got out that men were making millions digging silver in Leadville in 1878. Yet even when Womack made his second discovery in 1890, it can't be said that it paid off.

Yes, other men finally took notice when Womack wandered into Denver with saddlebags full of gold ore. And yes, the first prospectors began to trickle into Cripple Creek soon after, a small number of hopefuls willing to make a gamble. It could be called the first stage of the Cripple Creek gold rush—not that any of this would make a difference to Womack. Spending the next year digging for gold alongside the newly arrived prospectors, Womack's labors were just as fruitless as they had been for the long years before. Indeed, 1891 was a hard year for all the prospectors at Cripple Creek, so hard that the site was abandoned by all but the most stubborn. Womack himself finally decided he had had his fill of Cripple Creek; he sold his claim to a man named John P. Grannis for a mere $300. It would be a sale that Womack would regret for the rest of his life.

Later on that year, two men only remembered as Pat and Mike decided to try one more dig before they abandoned Cripple Creek. As a lark, the two men agreed that they would dig on the next spot that their dog stopped to relieve itself. It turned out that the dog's nose for gold was superior to theirs. Digging into the hard ground where their dog had just defecated, the pair promptly hit an enormous gold vein. Three weeks later, Pat and Mike dug out $100,000 in ore. The rush was on.

What Womack had sold for $300 was suddenly worth over a hundred times that. Overnight, Cripple Creek real estate became the hottest property in the United States as prospectors from every corner of the continent flooded into the region. Dance halls, gambling halls, hotels, saloons, parlor houses and flophouses seemed to spring from the very rock. By the end of 1892, over 10,000 people were living in Cripple Creek. The mining operations would last an incredibly long time by gold rush standards, with the last serious Cripple Creek mine closing down in 1961. Miners had dug up over 21 million ounces of gold from the Colorado earth in the nearly 70 years that Cripple Creek mines were active.

Today, scores of abandoned mines are littered throughout the Cripple Creek region, ghostly husks of expired industry that mark the location of subterranean tunnels long since gutted of any gold they once contained. If these old head-frames could talk, theirs would be tales of hardship, desperation and avarice—of tough men burrowing beneath the earth for mineral wealth, emerging from tunnels battered, bruised and beyond exhaustion, lucky, in the end, if they emerged at all. Indeed, far too many of these men would meet gruesome deaths while toiling under western ground. The Cripple Creek mines would kill many a gold digger before they were closed for good. And of all the lethal tunnels that were dug around Cripple Creek, the Mamie R. on Raven Hill became the most infamous.

Men who worked the Mamie R. knew there was something wrong from the very beginning. Early diggers would talk of the strange voices they heard in the depths. They spoke of voices that seemed to come from the very rock, coming at them from the damp darkness, sometimes low and guttural, other times high and tittering. Many tried to disregard the mysterious voices, explaining them away as echoes from other men in nearby tunnels. But there were also those miners who offered up far more disturbing explanations. Some of the men who worked the Mamie R. were mining veterans, men who had worked the coal seams in Cornwall and the pits of Cape Breton—men who were well acquainted with the denizens of the deep.

These miners were the ones who grew increasingly uneasy at the sounds in the Mamie R.'s tunnels. In hushed whispers they talked about the deathly creatures that wreaked so much havoc in other mines. "It's them knackers," they would say. "Creatures or spirits, no man can say for sure, but they live underground, hidden from the sun, and they've sent far too many good men to graves they didn't deserve. Make no mistake, there's evil in this mine."

Nevertheless, gold fever held the Mamie R. workers in such a thrall that few were all that worried about whispers in the dark. Until, that is, the accidents began to occur. The first tragedy happened in the early evening, when five men breaking gold ore off one of the tunnel walls were suddenly interrupted by one of their coworkers, a Texan by the name of Hank Bull. "Hold up for one second," the grimy miner called out to the others. "I swore I heard something down there."

Through the dim light of the hanging lanterns, the miners could see Hank's massive form standing very still in the tunnel. He was staring intently down the shaft. "What'd you hear down there, Hank?" one of the men asked.

"I heard a someone callin' my name."

"Down there?" another miner snorted. "Man, you been chewin' peyote? There ain't nothin' down there but more of this blasted rock. Now let's get back to work."

One of the men raised his pickax and was just about to let it fall when Hank stopped him. "Don't!" Hank snapped at the man with the raised pickax. "You guys must have heard *that*."

"Heard what?"

"That!" Hank said again, his head snapping toward some noise that none of the others could hear.

"What are you talkin' about, fool?"

"There's a boy down there, a little boy. He's calling out for me. You guys can't be telling me you don't hear him."

The conviction in Hank's voice was such that each of the miners stopped and listened carefully, their heads bent toward the tunnel. Long moments passed, but no one heard a sound from the shaft below, nothing but water dripping into gathering puddles and the occasional pebble rolling down the tunnel wall. "Nothin' there, Hank," one of the miners finally said. "Besides, how could there be? That stretch was just dug yesterday. No one would be foolish enough to go down there until the shaft is braced."

Hank was unmoved. "I'm going to take a gander for a second. I'll be back."

One of his coworkers called out to him, warning him that the tunnel ahead wasn't safe, that it hadn't been braced yet, but Hank gave no sign he heard as he disappeared down the tunnel. The miners all got quiet, listening to the sound of Hank Bull's boots fall on loose rock. Then there was nothing—not a sound. One minute passed, two minutes passed, and the miners were as still as statues in the absolute silence of the shaft, trying their best to fight a rising tide of fear. It seemed as if the water had stopped dripping; even the miners' labored breathing

rose and fell without a sound. And then, with a sudden-
ness that sent each of the men into spasms of terror, the
silence was broken by a horrifying scream. It was Hank,
his voice so fearful that it was almost unrecognizable.

Half the men jumped back to the tunnel entrance, the
other half leapt forward to help their distressed coworker,
but none of them made it very far before the tunnel
ahead caved in. The miners looked on helplessly as the
unsupported ceiling above Hank came down, burying the
hapless miner under a pile of rubble. Mamie R. workers
on the surface felt the earth rumble as rock dust billowed
from the mine entrance. The bucket was promptly lowered into the mine, and, one by one, each of the men was
brought out of the tunnels alive…except for Hank Bull.
The poor man was long dead when the workers finally
pulled his remains out of the tunnel. His body, smashed
and badly mangled, was almost unrecognizable, but it was
his face, twisted into an expression of the most profound
terror, which left the greatest impression on the men who
dug him out.

In daylight hours, very little was said about Hank's last
moments in the mine—the voice he claimed to hear, his
bloodcurdling scream just before the tunnel collapsed.
Yet the story of his demise circulated in whiskey-soaked
conversations and short whispers. All the while, the mysterious whispers and moving shadows continued within
the depths of the Mamie R., and it wasn't long before the
miners began deserting the eerie mine.

They left in droves, and soon only a skeleton crew
remained behind to mine the depths of the Mamie R.

Bold, stupid or just extraordinarily avaricious, these stubborn men stayed on even as the bizarre goings-on at the bottom of the mine got weirder. They dug deeper and deeper under Raven Hill, all the while ignoring the waxing strangeness that no one could explain.

Barely audible whispers in the dark turned into distinct voices, though no one could say what strange and guttural language the voices were speaking. Some claimed to see dark figures moving in their peripheral vision, figures that would vanish into the walls whenever the miners turned to get a better look. Not knowing what they were dealing with, the miners of the Mamie R. took to calling the beings in the dark "Tommyknockers" and did their best to work alongside them. The Tommyknockers, however, were not nearly so cooperative.

They seemed to take a special interest in the windlass system that transported men and ore from the tunnels to the surface. Men below would ring a signal bell three times to be hauled up above ground in the windlass bucket. Yet on too many occasions, the bell would be rung, the bucket would be hauled up, and nothing, neither men nor ore, would be there. If the miners were puzzled by this the first few times it occurred, they quickly grew accustomed to the skullduggery. "Damn Tommyknockers," miners would grumble. "Don't they have any respect for a man trying to earn his living?"

Before long, miners of the Mamie R. discovered that the Tommyknockers' malice ran much deeper than mere disrespect. The second death in the mine occurred in late November 1894 when a miner standing at the bottom of the entrance shaft had his skull crushed by the windlass bucket, which had come loose of the cable and had plummeted down the pit. Although all in the Mamie R. mourned the death of another miner, no one could explain how the bucket had come loose; the windlass rope was still intact and the knot that was tied to the bucket was still fastened tight. Given the evidence, there was no way the bucket could have come loose. If any of the men working the mine had gotten used to the Tommyknockers, this incident hardened their hatred of those mysterious creatures in the mine.

In turn, the strange happenings in the mine increased dramatically. Some miners claimed that they could hear the Tommyknockers closer than ever, as if they were standing right next to them, whispering unintelligible threats into their ears. Anyone turning to get a look at these creatures would find nothing there but the damp darkness of the Mamie R. It did not stop there. At the end of the workday, many exhausted miners claimed to catch glimpses of small, horned creatures no more than three feet tall dashing about in obvious glee, celebrating the miners' departure by leaping to and fro in some sort of demented dance. It was always dark when the miners caught sight of these creatures, and though no one claimed to see them clearly, they always described them the same: short, with two horns jutting out of their heads and burning, red eyes.

Whether the Tommyknockers were getting bolder as the miners dug deeper or had simply grown tired of the miners' presence might not ever be known, but in the weeks after the second miner's death, the feeling in the Mamie R. became almost intolerable. In addition to the now near-constant hiss of angry voices and darting shadows, some miners claimed to see the bleeding apparitions of their recently departed coworkers. A badly injured Hank Bull was seen in the deepest recesses of the mine, walking through the tunnels with a completely expressionless look on his bleeding face. Men hoisting the windlass bucket out of the mine at the sound of the signal bell would stand back in terror as the apparition of the second dead miner would silently emerge from the shaft, his blank eyes staring listlessly from his crushed skull. Moving to get out of the bucket, the wounded apparition would vanish the moment its foot touched the surface.

And still, the men of the Mamie R. remained resolute, digging the ore out from the tunnel walls without complaint. Until, that is, Christmas Day 1894, a few short weeks after the second miner was killed, when another miner was killed in another freakish accident. The circumstances of this death were so improbable, and so absolutely gruesome, that every man in the Mamie R. abandoned the mine, never to return.

The Mamie R. had flooded on Christmas Eve, and the miners had spent most of the next day hauling water out of the tunnels, one bucket at a time. There were three men working the windlass on the surface, hoisting buckets of water out of the shaft as they were filled. It happened in all of an instant. The windlass, groaning under the weight of the buckets of water, suddenly came apart: the winding spool that the rope was wrapped around flew off the frame, causing a dozen yards of rope to come loose as the bucket full of water plummeted down the shaft. One of the men on the surface had become entangled in the slack rope, which was quickly snaking down the well along with the bucket. Then the line snapped taught, cleanly decapitating the man who had been draped in the rope. Apparently, a coil had settled on his shoulders, and when the rope was pulled tight by the force of the falling bucket, it sliced through his neck like a razor-sharp knife. No one tried to explain how the winding spool had come off the windlass. The miners had had enough; convinced that the Tommyknockers were responsible for the three fatal accidents in the mine, every one of the miners quit that Christmas. Word of the cursed Mamie R. spread throughout Cripple Creek, and no one from the mining community would replace the workers. By late January 1895, the mine beneath Raven Hill was officially closed—its depths were never plumbed for gold again.

Although the story of the Mamie R. mine has become a legend in the ghostlore of the West, Colorado's State Bureau of Mines has no record that it ever existed. Skeptics have used this fact to debunk the story of the Mamie R. If every other mine that was dug in the Cripple Creek region is listed, why not the alleged Mamie R.? The response has come with the argument that the Mamie R. operated only until 1894, and the bureau's census of the Cripple Creek began one year later, in 1895. Being one of the few mines that closed before the bureau took its census, it was never included in the bureau's books, and thus was lost in the historical record.

And so it is—as it is with many such legends—that belief depends more upon gut feeling and faith than any immutable proof. Were the Tommyknockers in the Mamie R. one and the same as the "Knackers" of Cornish legend, alive and well under American earth? If so, what, exactly, were they? Subterranean beasts with a fierce dislike for humanity? Or perhaps evil or disconsolate spirits awoken by miners' pickaxes and dynamite? No one knows for sure. Some have guessed that the Mamie R. might have been situated on an Indian burial ground, and the Tommyknockers were Indian spirits angered at having their rest disturbed on account of gold diggers' greed. Others have likened the Tommyknockers to goblins and kobolds, mythic European creatures that have a natural hatred for humans. Whatever the case, if the Tommyknockers do indeed exist under Cripple Creek, and if they are every amount as vicious as the legend of the Mamie R. would have us believe, it is probably a case of the less we know, the better.

The Dunn Building

The town of Victor was incorporated in 1893, given life by the surge of miners that came flooding into the Cripple Creek region looking for gold. Located just a few miles south of the town of Cripple Creek, Victor soon came to be the economic heart of the gold mining region, surpassing Cripple Creek itself as the busiest town in the area. Like so many other mining towns across the West that mushroomed overnight, however, Victor mostly grew in unsavory directions during its formative years.

The ratio of saloons to churches in 1893 was high enough that every drifter for miles around with an affinity for depravity and an aversion to decency might want to pay the town a visit. Surely the badly outnumbered peace officers in town would have sworn this to be true. In 1893, the streets of Victor were crawling with every sort of bad man in the West: gamblers, gunfighters, murderers, madmen, bushwhackers, wolfers, conmen and, amongst these all, miners—all armed, all inebriated and all congregated in the smoky saloons that made a brisk trade off their vices. It didn't take very long for Victor's Boot Hill to become dense with pine box residents.

Indeed, Victor's morticians were almost as busy as its barkeepers, and of them all, Thomas Dunn was the busiest. He practiced his trade in the Dunn Building, enjoying a rather macabre heyday during the town's early years. His was one of the first funeral parlors in town. By all accounts, although swamped with corpses during Victor's first years, Dunn was said to be the consummate professional, able to make bullet holes and mortal wounds virtually invisible on the cadavers that were brought to him. Bloodied gunfighters came out of Dunn's funeral parlor looking like posthumous gentlemen. Miners who had come to tragic and gruesome deaths in the tunnels around town were laid to rest without any visible trace of their horrible wounds.

Given that Dunn worked with the dead throughout his life, it might not come as such a surprise that strange stories about the Dunn Building abounded after the famed mortician passed away. Paranormal enthusiasts might even say that supernatural activity could be expected, considering the number of dead bodies that went in and out of the building.

When Mrs. Dunn turned the building into a boarding house after Mr. Dunn passed away, there was no shortage of stories offered by boarders who stayed on the second floor of the boarding house. Residents told of sudden cold spots that would come out of nowhere, making the hair on the back of their necks stand on end. Others heard heavy footsteps slowly making their way through rooms and sometimes down the second floor hallway, though not a man, woman or child was visible to the eye.

There were more chilling stories. Some boarders left the Dunn Building in the middle of the night, babbling hysterically about how they were woken by a terrible suffocating feeling. They said it was as if some invisible force of incredible strength was pressing down on their lungs, and only when they bolted from bed and out of their rooms were they able to breathe again. Others claimed that a pair of invisible hands, freezing and as hard as stone, had wrapped themselves around their throats while they were trying to sleep, strangling the breath out of them for several terrifying moments before suddenly releasing them. Although no one was ever physically hurt by the spirits that haunted the Dunn Building, there was more than one frightened boarder who would attest to their maliciousness.

For the longest time, people just assumed the spirits of those bitterly departed that once went in and out of the funeral parlor were responsible for the goings-on in the Dunn Building. Until 1899, that is, when a man who had been one of Mr. Dunn's assistants spoke up about a disturbing incident that took place in the funeral home in 1893. His tale shed new light on the events in the old funeral parlor.

According to this man's story, it happened while Dunn was working on the corpse of a miner who had been badly mutilated in a cave-in. He had just begun preparing the miner for burial when the supposed cadaver suddenly twitched on the embalming table. A moment later, the badly bleeding body came to tortured life; one of its hands darted out to grab the startled mortician while the other reached up to feel the remnants of its mangled face. It was an undertaker's nightmare come true: the dead man on the table wasn't quite dead yet.

The realization hit the mortician, his assistant and the supposed-to-be-dead miner with equal force. As Dunn took a few horrified steps backward, the man on the table let out a bloodcurdling wail and tried to sit up. Although the miner did manage to get up, it quickly became obvious he didn't know which way to go; he couldn't see a thing through his one remaining eye. Another frightful shriek split through the confines of the undertaker's office.

"He's delirious with pain!" Dunn yelled to his assistant over the miner's agonized wails. "Get me the morphine!"

The young man ran for the painkiller as Dunn did his best to restrain the flailing erstwhile corpse. It wasn't until they had filled the miner's veins with morphine that he finally settled down, falling in a heap on the mortuary floor. After picking him up and putting him back on the embalming table, Dunn's assistant turned to go get help, but he was stopped by his employer before he was able to take a single step toward the door. "Where the hell you think you're going?" Dunn grunted at his assistant, wiping the miner's blood off his face and hands.

The assistant looked at Dunn uncomprehendingly, still shocked, uncertain of how to respond. "He isn't dead; he needs a doctor."

"Doctor!" Dunn roared. "Look at this man. What do you think a doctor could possibly do for him?"

The young man froze in his tracks. His eyes fell on the moaning man lying on the embalming table. "What would you have me do?"

Dunn looked at his assistant for a moment before giving his response. "Get more morphine. We'll put him to rest."

Barely hesitating, Dunn's assistant did as he was told and filled another syringe with the drug. Dunn himself delivered the lethal injection and hardly waited at all before resuming his work on the miner. The young assistant couldn't help noticing that the miner was still producing a faint pulse while he was being prepared for burial.

Nevertheless, the assistant undertaker kept quiet about the affair for years, confessing the grisly deed only after the funeral parlor was turned into a boarding house and the ghost of the Dunn Building became widely known. But he didn't stop at this confession. He also told Mrs. Dunn that ever since the miner was put to death, strange things began to happen at the funeral parlor. The undertaker and his assistant became conscious of an intangible presence, malevolent and unseen, which wandered through the building. Sometimes they could hear him— his footsteps making their way across the second floor when they knew they were the only two living people in the building. On other occasions they would feel him— his icy presence, angry and hateful, filling both of them with silent dread. As soon as Mr. Dunn died, his assistant quit the business and never once ventured back into the Dunn Building; it seems the spirit of the angry miner enjoyed no such luxury of leaving.

The legend of the Dunn Building is one of those stories that refuses to die, told and retold by generation after generation. To this day, psychics and paranormal investigators who have investigated the building in Victor will adamantly state that a malevolent spirit still drifts through its halls, just as angry as it ever was. Perhaps the miner is convinced that he might have been saved if someone put him in front of a doctor instead of a mortician so many years ago.

The German and the Body in the Bucket

History has forgotten his name. In fact, his name was quite probably never known from the outset. It certainly wasn't reported in the August 8, 1879 edition of the *Central City Daily Register*, in which the man in question is referred to only as "the German." A German, it should be added, who was a newcomer in Leadville during that mining town's silver boom. A German, it should also be added, who was a miner recently employed by one of the big companies that had moved in to do business in the burgeoning silver town.

Now this German did not know it, but he was hired on to work this particular shaft because a miner had just recently lost his life working its depths. For it was, and continues to be, one of the terrible truths of the profession: where there are mines, there are men who die working them. Miners have always faced myriad dangers, and no matter how much safety regulations improve, death in the depths has always been a looming specter.

Still, this specter loomed much larger in 19th-century boomtowns such as Leadville, where the rush to make a quick buck took precedence over all other concerns, including the safety of the men who plumbed the depths for mineral wealth. As far as the companies were concerned, labor was the cheapest commodity. When a man died under the mountain, there would always be another man willing to take his place.

In early August 1879, a man died in the bottom of a Leadville shaft when a support beam failed and a section of the tunnel caved in, crushing him to death instantly. In accordance with tradition, the miner was somberly lifted from the shaft, then promptly replaced at the first opportunity.

The German was the unfortunate man's replacement, arriving in Leadville a few days after the accident. His English was not very good and he had no references in town, but it was obvious by the calluses on his hands, the muscles of his shoulders and the hardness in his eyes that he knew well the places where men moil beneath the earth, and he was hired on the spot. Because he did not need to know the fate of the man he replaced, no one told him. But he would find out on his own soon enough.

It would be his first and last descent into the mine. They lowered him down to the bottom of the shaft; he had been down for no more than minute when the rope began to shake vigorously—trouble. "What is it, Fritz!" one of the men on the surface shouted down, using a nickname that might have stuck if the German had.

The shouted response echoed up against the shaft walls; the fear in his voice was apparent to the men on the surface. "*Mein Gott!* Zere is a man here! Kaput! On ze ground! He is dead!"

"A man?" said one of the men up top. "Don't tell me another fella gone and died down there."

Silence followed, up on the surface and down below. Then: "Vel, zen, what ze hell vould you have me do wit zis?"

The men at the top chuckled despite themselves. "Poor Fritz," one of them said. "First day on the job and he's got to run into a dead man down there."

"Ain't no way to start, that's for sure," said another.

There was another round of laughter from the rough men up top before the senior man decided to speak up. "It's all right, Fritz, yer probably jus' lookin' at some fool drunk who fell down the shaft last night. Stick around long enough and you'll see a few more. Ain't no need to panic, just put the man in the bucket and we'll pull 'im up. Y'hear?"

The German shouted the affirmative. There was the sound of shuffling down below, the miner grunting as he labored with the weight of the dead man, then three jerks on the rope. "Okay!" came the holler up the tunnel. "Pull him up!"

The men on the surface took the weight, mimicking their new coworker's accent as they turned the windlass. "Pull him up! Pull him up!" one man laughed.

"All right, Fritz, easy does it. Where's the fire?" said another.

This was all bravado, a desperate attempt to talk over the prevailing uneasiness, the thought of what the men would see when the bucket reached the surface. They had all seen their fair share of corpses over the years, but it never got easier. Who was it? A young man? Old? Someone any of them knew? One of the men at the windlass broke the tense silence: "Anyone know about any drunks wanderin' around here last night?"

"Could be anyone," came the senior miner's gruff voice.

The trepidation on the surface was such that the men on the windlass did not notice a very peculiar development. At first, when they had begun to haul up the dreaded contents of the bucket, the weight at the end of the line was significant, and it was with no small effort that they hauled it up. Yet as the rope coiled around the windlass, as the bucket slowly rose up the shaft, the weight grew lighter. And it continued to do so as the bucket climbed. The effect was so gradual that the men did not take any notice of it, each of them attributing it to the increased efforts of the other. Only when the bucket was very near the top of the shaft did it strike them as odd. The bucket was weightless; the windlass turned easily. They wondered for the first time if they were hauling up anything at all.

They got their answer a moment later, when the bucket was pulled to the surface—without anything inside. Completely empty. There was a moment of surprised silence, followed by a raucous round of laughter. "Good one, Fritz!" the senior minter roared down the shaft. "A dead man! Sure! And here we were thinking you were some humorless Kraut! Showed us!" The man paused and scowled. "But don't make a habit out of this nonsense! We're here to work, not fool on each other."

The only men who remained uneasy were the men at the windlass, who recalled how heavy the bucket was when they had begun pulling; and, of course, the German, who, for the life of him, could not understand what was so funny about a corpse in a bucket. *Have zey gone mad?* he thought in the darkness below. *Zis country is full of lunatics. Mein Gott, vy did I ever leave ze Fatherland?*

Perturbed as he was, the German continued down below. Like the men above, he was a seasoned miner who had seen men die on the job, and he refused to let a dead body keep him from his work. He was here to dig, after all, and was conscious of the fact that he would have to prove his mettle to his new coworkers.

It was not until he returned back to the surface, some hours later, that he came to know the cause of the laughter. "So that dead man in the bucket gag was good for a laugh," the senior miner said, approaching him as he wiped off the grime of the shaft. "But we won't be having anymore such tomfoolery, y'hear?"

The German was confused. "Vatever do you mean?"

"Vatever do *you* mean, Fritz," snickered one of the other miners, imitating his coworker's accent. Oh, the fun they were going to have with this one.

"But zere was a man in ze tunnel," the German protested. "I saw him wit my own eyes. I dragged him to ze bucket!"

"Sure there was, Fritz," another miner grunted. "It was a good one, fer sure. But ye gotta know where to draw the line. Joke's over."

"Vat joke? Zere is no joke! I carried ze man into ze bucket!"

The senior miner looked hard at his new miner, trying to figure out what to make of this man, how to deal with him. Had he lost his mind? He'd worked with crazy men before. Hell, some of the best miners he knew played with a few cards short. That wasn't a problem. But if this German *was* crazy, he would need to know, that was all. "Boys," the senior miner barked at the men who had been at the windlass. "What did you see in the bucket? Was there anything in the bucket?"

There was a silence, as the men recalled how heavy the bucket had been at first and how it became weightless by the time they pulled it out of the ground. "Well, just like you, boss, we didn't see nuthin' in the bucket," one of the men said. "But ye know, at first, it was real heavy-like. When we *first* started pullin', no doubt that it felt like there was somethin' in there. I would've sworn it." The other men on the windlass nodded their assent.

"That's a fact," said an elderly miner.

"You see! You see!" cried the German. "Zere *vas* a dead man at ze bottom. Zey pulled him up!"

The senior miner nodded his head warily. "All right, all right, don't get yerself worked up. There ought to be an explanation for all this."

But by this point, the German insisted on being heard. "He vas as real as me or you!" he continued. "He had black hair viz curls, and a beard. His body vas crushed by rock, and his shirt vas brown viz red stripes." The German was ranting now. "His socks vere different colors as vell. Von vas black, and ze ozer vas gray. He vore a chain on his neck. It had on it a cross and a nugget of gold."

The German was so preoccupied with his tirade that he did not notice that he had won all the miners' undivided attention. They had all fallen silent right around the time he had described the shirt the dead man had been wearing, their stunned disbelief culminating in the German's description of the chain.

"What the hell you talkin' about, Fritz?" one of the men finally asked.

"You have any idea who it is ye just went ahead and described?" the senior miner added, his voice measured and dangerous. The burly old man looked around at the rest of his crew, then. "Anyone tell this Kraut about what happened down there?"

Silence was their response. Some of the men silently shook their heads. The mining boss knew it was a ridiculous question. He did not have to ask. He knew his men; none of them would have said anything.

The German surveyed the strangers sitting before him. "Tell me about vat?" he asked, though the pit in his stomach was telling him that he probably did not want to know. "Vat happened down in zere?"

"A man died down there," the old miner barked. "The man you just described was him. We dug alongside that tough son of a gun for years, and he never went anywhere without that cross around his neck, that cross with a piece of gold he dug up in Deadwood. There ain't one of us who hadn't heard that damned story a million times. About the time he'd been panning fer nuthin' fer weeks, stopped and said a heartfelt prayer, and that nugget rolled right by 'im."

One of the men snickered at the memory of their lost coworker. "Damn fool," he said.

"That damn fool is who ye just told us about, Fritz," the senior miner said. "Right down to his shirt and socks, that was him. Now what d'you have to say about that?"

But the German had nothing to say. As far as he was concerned, he was done with this crew—done, as a matter of fact, with the entire town of Leadville. Cutting through underground tunnels, liable to collapse at any moment, he could handle. He could also handle the rough company of men who engaged in the same activity. He could cope with the oh-so-predictable nickname, the cracks about his accent. But what he could *not* deal with was the idea of sharing a tunnel with the ghost of a dead man— especially with the knowledge that he had been hired to replace him. The German left town the next day, but the mining outfit apparently had no problems continuing on in their claim. They simply went into the nearest saloon and picked another man willing to dig. Perhaps it was merely a matter of the former miner having something against Germans, for nothing more was ever written or said of a bleeding apparition lying in the bottom of the shaft.

3
Haunted
Railways

The Woman on the Timpas Tracks

No one could say how long she had been there. Some say ever since there had been a train line cutting through Otero County. No one was able to say, either, what her name was, where she came from or why. She came from nowhere, as mysterious as she was unsettling. Still, there was one thing that could be said: for as long as she was there, there were also eager engineers, men who drove their trains as fast as they were able through the town of Timpas, hoping, praying even, that she would be there on the tracks, waiting.

As much of a mystery as she was, any man who saw her was never able to forget her—tall and graceful with long red hair, she would emerge from the darkness of the windblown prairie dressed in flowing white. The sight of her glowing in the locomotive light caused more than one engine driver to gasp in shock, and not just at her extraordinary beauty. For when she appeared, she was never more than a few yards from the oncoming train, far too close for the engineer to stop in time.

It was a terrifying experience for an engineer who had never seen her before, certainly. But one who had the presence of mind to look a little closer would see that the woman his train was about to hit showed not a trace of fear at the imminent collision. Rather, she wore a brilliant smile, and in the instant that the train was about to hit, she would open her arms to the huffing iron horse, spreading them wide to embrace it.

The terrified engineer could only watch as, instead of pulverizing the woman in white, the train passed straight through her as if she were nothing more than a wisp of smoke. Then, in the next horrifying moment, the woman would be in the locomotive, mere inches from the speechless engine driver, with the same brilliant smile on her face. She would step closer, and the fear would be replaced by something else—a need to swallow hard and difficulty breathing. It was impossible that she was even there, but that fact was somehow forgotten. Something else took precedence: the woman's beauty, and how close she was standing. These thoughts would be foremost in a bewildered engineer's mind. Her flirtatious smile did not help matters, and she would step forward again, now far too close to whatever poor and sooty engineer was standing there before her.

What happened next would depend on who was telling the story. Some engineers have said the woman in white leaned forward and kissed them before vanishing into thin air. Others enjoyed more of her time. Or at least this was a claim the more boastful engineers enjoyed making. "Lookin' as though the lady likes some of us more than others," went the laughing refrain. "One man gets a 'how do you do' while another gets somethin' else all together." Readers can guess what this "somethin' else" was.

There were other accounts as well. The engineers of the Atchison, Topeka & Santa Fe line liked to say that they were the reason the woman in white appeared on the tracks, but according to a number of other versions of the legend, the stunning, redheaded woman was just as interested in the passengers as she was the engine men.

More than once in the latter half of the 1800s, travelers on the line in question were shocked awake by the sudden appearance of a woman in white drifting down the aisle of one of the passenger cars. Her description matched the woman who had bewitched the engineers in the front of the train—dressed in white with long red hair and an alluring smile. She would appear for no longer than a minute or two before vanishing from sight. Further, she was said to appear at about the same place along the track: in Otero County, just past the town of Timpas. There was one notable difference between the engineers' encounters and those in the passenger compartments, however; none of the rail users claimed to share the same level of intimacy as the engine men.

Maybe it was that she had a real affinity for railway men, or perhaps the suggestive exchanges railway men boasted of were nothing more than wishful thinking. Whatever the case—whether she was a flirtatious spirit or merely the ghost of a young woman who once had a penchant for trains—there was one thing that could be said: she had a special preference for the Atchison, Topeka & Santa Fe line that ran through Otero County, especially in the place where it passed through Timpas.

Stories of the woman in white persisted throughout the 19th century. Seen on numerous occasions by startled passengers and prurient engineers alike, she was at once a lonely spirit in need of a man's company and a friendly ghost that enjoyed being on trains. But how she had come to haunt that stretch of track, and what, if anything, her smiling spirit was trying to say, was anyone's guess.

There was the predictable speculation that she was the spirit of a woman who had died on the tracks outside of Timpas, but then there was no record of any such thing happening. Further, although she had been spotted many times on the train through Timpas, no one had ever seen her on the ground. Indeed, the only time she was ever visible outside the train was in that handful of seconds when she was on the tracks in front of the locomotive, just before she was hit.

Whoever she was, sightings of the woman in white have long since ceased. All but forgotten in the 20th century, she has become one of the folktales rooted in the American countryside—a railroad version of the innumerable phantom hitchhiker stories scattered over the highways of the nation. And just like the subjects of so many of those tragic tales, the woman on the tracks in Otero County is as much of a mystery. She began appearing on those Colorado tracks without cause or purpose, only to stop without hint of an explanation—another inexplicable addition to the country's vast canon of supernatural folklore.

The Specter at the Station House

People were generally able to agree on two things about the apparition at the Burlington and Missouri station house of Lafayette—it was big, and it was white. They differed on pretty well everything else. One of the first accounts, covered in the March 10, 1893 edition of *The Denver Republican*, tells of a station house employee who was so startled the apparition's sudden appearance that he drew his revolver and shot at it. Shot at it six times over, it ought to be added. Although the shooting spree left the white figure unscathed, the trigger-happy employee did manage to shatter every window in the station house and, while he was at it, make the figure in white into something of a local sensation in the small town of Lafayette.

In this initial report, the ghost was described as "white, about seven feet high, broad shouldered and heavy chested." A vague description, certainly, that left a lot open to the imagination. Was it a glowing white figure? Or just a big person dressed in white? "Seven feet high, broad shouldered and heavy chested" seems to suggest that this figure was a freakishly large man, but was this known? What did the figure's face look like? Or was there anything to see at all?

None of these questions were answered by eyewitnesses at the second sighting, where, despite the presence of 12 townsfolk, not another descriptive word about the figure emerged in the article about the apparition. What was made clear was that the apparition had a way of striking fear in the hearts of men and women alike. It was written in the same newspaper article that all who saw it "felt a cold, frigid feeling in their backs," while "the city marshal became paralyzed, and his hat was lifted from his head."

What was this thing? Where did it come from and why? These were questions that everyone in Lafayette seemed to be asking that March, and there seemed to be as many responses as there were people who had claimed to see it. It was a towering, formless mass emitting a palpable feeling of dread. It was an enormous, featureless outline, obviously a man, standing threateningly in the middle of the station house, confronting everyone present with an unspoken challenge.

Apparently, it was a challenge that some terrified eyewitnesses took seriously. The employee who emptied his revolver on that March 10 evening was not the only one who thought about shooting at it. A bullet-ridden front door was added to the shot-out windows when the specter appeared before a lone passenger waiting for a night train to arrive. According to this man, the massive shape appeared suddenly, standing well over seven feet tall and emitting a shimmering, silver light. The man did not need to think about what he was looking at. He just knew, by the cold in his spine and the fear in his heart, that the thing in front of him was not good—that it meant harm. He reacted automatically, yanking his six-shooter out of its holster and opening up on the menacing apparition. The slugs passed right through the white shape and into the heavy front door of the station house. The white shape, unaffected by the shower of lead, lingered on for a few more minutes before vanishing.

All these events whipped the Lafayette citizenry into a modest frenzy; the town was abuzz with word of what was going on at the station house. People spoke of a monstrous ghost out at the depot that showed up right at the stroke of midnight. According to some, it was a vicious spirit that attacked two men, who saved themselves only by their speed with their six-shooters. Others spoke about how the figure was an omen of death, and all who looked upon it were doomed to die before the end of the year. The town's religious crowd steeled themselves for the second coming. And everyone, *everyone*, headed out to the station house to take a look for themselves.

There was another sighting in the same week that the goings-on at the station were featured in *The Denver Republican*. Lafayette residents had been heading out in droves nightly, but the white figure had kept a low profile after the employee had shot out the windows. It was not until it occurred to a number of residents to try showing up at another time that they were rewarded with another sighting. Up until then, most of the eager spectators had been arriving just before midnight, having been told that the figure only made its appearance when the clock chimed 12.

No one could say how this rumor originated, but as it turned out, it was false. The second time the apparition was sighted by a large crowd, it was at exactly nine o'clock in the evening. There were a number of residents milling around in the waiting room when the front door swung open and a brilliant white apparition strode in among them. This time there were several careful observers in the crowd, and a description emerged in the pages of *The Denver Republican* the next day: "The ghost is described by one who was within 10 feet of it as being that of a woman, whose neck and shoulders were bare. The features could be distinctly seen."

Needless to say, this article raised quite a furor. The looming white figure, which had caused more than one man to cower in fear, was actually a woman? Furthermore, she appeared to be a woman who did not mean any harm. No one who saw her on this occasion felt threatened in any way. Rather, they stood watching in awe as this luminous figure walked by all of them slowly and with perfect grace. She paused for a moment at the foot of the stairs, looked back, smiled and began climbing to the second floor. Becoming more and more transparent with every step, she vanished altogether before she reached the top.

In light of this latest sighting, the tales circulating about the station house haunting changed considerably. No longer a menacing, "broad shouldered and heavy-chested," seven-foot apparition who prompted men to pull their guns, the Lafayette ghost took on the sadder tones of tragedy. She was the spirit of a woman who had died at the station a few years back when she fell upon the tracks just as a train was pulling in.

Once the story was revised, an early, previously unknown sighting of the sad apparition became public when a proud mother stepped forward with her daughter in tow, claiming that her girl had seen the woman a few months ago. Her mother had been right there with her at the time, but not seeing the glimmering "white lady" her daughter was describing, had chalked it up to a child's imagination and left it at that. Now she was presenting her daughter as a prescient medium, able to see things before they were visible to everyone else.

Although this woman never got very far on such claims, the talk of the spirit at the station house continued. Interestingly enough, the crowds at the station thinned considerably after the phantom there was said to be not so sinister. Ghosts of graceful women peacefully ascending staircases are not nearly as sensational as towering apparitions confronting armed men.

Such a wide variation in the sightings of the same purported phenomenon, and within the span of such a short time—when it comes to ghosts, this is more typical than many readers might realize. It is one of the reasons that so many rational minds greet ghost stories with skepticism. Generally, the more famous a haunting, the greater the number of conflicting accounts there are about it. Where ghosts are concerned, there are usually people unable to agree on the facts.

As for what to believe (if anything) in the case of the Lafayette station house, it is impossible to say. Today the station no longer stands, and besides, sightings of the white apparition were reduced to next-to-none shortly after the furor died down in 1893. Assuming, for a moment, that the entire affair was not fabricated by sensational reporting and residents' over-active imaginations, the two men who felt compelled to open fire upon sighting the apparition were alone when it appeared and, being among the first to see it, may have been blinded enough with terror to invent the massive menace so zealously described in the paper. As for the group sighting that largely corroborated these men's claims, much has been said about the power of suggestion, and we might imagine the way a frightened rumor could turn the appearance of a ghostly woman into a dreadful apparition. Who can say for sure? In the end, it may have even been that there were two spirits at the Lafayette station house: one an enraged monster, the other a smiling woman. As is usually the case where the supernatural is concerned, we must be content with supposition.

The Ghost of Essie Mentzer

There were three people waiting at the platform as the late train chugged into the Telluride depot. One was a broad-shouldered young man who, just that morning, had realized that he'd seen enough of the mines in the San Juan. Deciding to quit his moiling under the mountains mere minutes after the realization sunk in, he gathered what money he had managed to save, downed one last shot of Colorado rotgut, wiped the grime off his face and headed to the train station. *Going back to sweet Chicago,* he thought, *where makin' a living don't mean buryin' yerself alive with a pickax in one hand and a lantern in the other.*

The other man was middle aged, thin and bespectacled, dressed in a checkered suit with a worn bowler hat over his hairless head and a black band around his bony arm. A saloon owner who was loathe to leave his business in the hands of his bartender, he had been obliged to buy his ticket back east after receiving the telegram that informed him of his mother's passing. *About time, vicious old hag,* he thought when he had read the news. But she was still his mother, and he would never forgive himself if he did not show up for her burial.

Occupied as they were with their thoughts, both ex-miner and grieving saloon owner found themselves distracted by the third person waiting at the platform. It was not just that she was a beautiful, young woman, but that she was so visibly distraught. Seemingly unaware of the two men there with her, she was staring at the approaching train with pleading eyes, looking as though she would give the world if only to quicken its arrival. But it was when she threw those looks over her shoulder, looking back in a state of near panic, that the two men got a sense of just how desperate she was.

The fact that he was getting on a train with someone who was obviously running away from something did not make the saloon owner happy. *Probably a workin' girl that went and did somethin' stupid,* he thought, sneering. *Maybe killed some poor bloke 'cause he didn't tip her. Wouldn't be surprised one damn bit if the law shows up any time now.*

The former miner was possessed of a more chivalrous disposition and found himself wishing there was some way he could come to the aid of the distraught young woman. He stood there at the platform, his gaze going from the approaching train to the woman, seesawing over possible courses of action. He thought: *I should go over and ask her what's the matter.* Then: *Aw, c'mon now, that's plain old untoward. She'll tell me to take a hike, is what. I should mind my own business is what I should do.* And then back to: *But I should go over and ask her what's the matter.* Despite all the deliberation, the young man just stood there, doing his best not to stare.

The train came to a screeching halt, and the three passengers boarded—the young woman, anxiously, followed by the young man, politely, followed by the saloon owner, reluctantly. The woman's anxiety did not lessen once she set foot in the passenger car. If anything, her mood seemed to worsen. Walking down the aisle, she kept looking back in near-terror, as though she were afraid someone else might be boarding.

The young man resisted the urge to put a comforting hand on her shoulder. *Anyone gets on this train and tries to mess with her, they've got something coming, that's fer sure.*

Meanwhile, the saloon owner was hoping the law would arrive before the train departed. *Woman's done something wrong, ain't no doubt. I'd do something about this if I was half the man I was 20 years ago.* He eyed the broad-shouldered miner reproachfully.

The train east was crowded, and the trio ended up sitting near one another as the whistle blew and the locomotive lurched back to life. Both men now had their eyes fixed on the woman, curious to see her reaction. She was on her way out of Telluride. Whatever she was running from, it was doubtful now that it would catch up with her any time soon—certainly not on this journey.

But it quickly became obvious that the woman was taking little comfort from the fact that wheels were moving under them. In fact, if anything, as the train picked up speed she seemed to grow even more anxious. Both the ex-miner and the saloon owner were asking themselves what was wrong with this woman. And they were not the only ones asking the question.

The young woman was attracting attention. Muttering to herself, wringing her hands, her worried gaze darting back and forth between her window and the entrance to the passenger car, she began to make the people around her nervous.

"What's wrong with that girl?" one woman was heard whispering to her husband.

"What do you think?" a retired soldier said to his traveling companion. "She know something the rest of us don't? Indian attack? Bandits?"

The woman continued to grow increasingly anxious, despite the effect it was having on her fellow travelers. When the train really picked up steam, she put her head into her hands and began to weep openly. A buzz formed around her, and it was then that the ex-miner finally found the courage to speak up. "Excuse me, miss," the young man said, drawing close so as to shield her from the curious gazes crowding in. "I know it isn't any of my business, and all, but I couldn't help but notice you're right uneasy about somethin'. Is there anything I can do to help?"

The woman looked up at him, then, her terrified eyes pooling up with tears. "Can't you see? He's coming for me."

The ex-miner was taken aback by the fear in her voice. "Who would that be, miss? We're well out of Telluride by now, and if there's anybody on this train that means you harm, well, there's some men here that won't let that happen—believe you me."

The saloon owner was sitting across from the two, and he could not help but sneer at the young man's words. But it wasn't until the ex-miner made his next avowal, that he, *personally*, would not allow anything to happen to her, that, despite his better judgment, the saloon owner finally spoke up. And when he did, it was with a sneer. "What you thinkin'? Boy yer age oughta know better'n to stick his nose in another's business. For all you know, this lady of yers is runnin' from the law!"

Now everyone sitting nearby was turning to look at the strapping young man with the reddening face, the gaunt saloon owner with the black armband and the beautiful yet obviously terrified woman. Necks craned; whispers went up and down the passenger car.

The ex-miner, painfully aware of all the attention, spoke his next words through gritted teeth. "Harm was never done in askin' a lady if she's in need of help," he said.

This struck the saloon owner as one of the funniest things he had ever heard. "Is that a fact?" he said, laughing loud enough for everyone to hear. "Whoever told you that one really pulled one over on ya. My experience is there's nuthin' more dangerous than a lady in need of help."

As the two men argued, the lady in question looked completely oblivious to the fact that she had become the subject of the heated exchange. But her fear, now visible to all, seemed to be getting worse with every mile. She saw enemies everywhere. Her wide, terror-filled eyes darted from face to face before going back to the window, searching for some mysterious doom in the darkness. She was ignoring the two men, whose loud words were getting louder.

"You don't know the first thing about this lady, so why don't you keep your judgment to yourself," the miner said, his voice taking on a dangerous timbre.

"Well she's sitting right there, why don't you ask her yerself?" the saloon owner replied. Passengers were openly staring now, watching the scene unfold—some with curiosity, some with concern, some with amusement.

The flustered young man finally risked a long look at the woman he was so concerned about. Apparently still lost in her own anxiety, it appeared that she had missed everything that had just transpired. *How can she be sitting right here and not hear us talkin' about her all this time?* Even he, who wanted to believe the best of her, found this hard to swallow. "Uh, miss? Hello, miss? Me and my, er…" he glared at the saloon owner. "Me and my colleague, here, couldn't help but notice that you're looking a tad bit bothered. Is everything okay?"

When she did not respond, when she did not even look at the man, the saloon owner lost his patience. "Excuse me, young lady!" he exploded, reaching out to grab her. "The young gentleman here asked you a question! Or are you too good to…" he was not able to finish. For the moment his hand touched her shoulder, he recoiled in shock and pulled back his arm, his stunned look going from his hand to the woman sitting in front of him. "Who are you?" he whispered in wonder.

As for the woman, the saloon keeper's touch seemed to snap her out of her anxious trance. She looked at the man in front of her as though she were seeing him for the first time. "Please, sir," she whispered. "Have you seen *him* yet? My heart tells me that he will not let me get away this easily. I fear he's still coming for me."

The saloon owner ignored her question and repeated his own; staring at her in shock, he cupped the hand that had touched her and hissed, "Who are you?"

A married couple who had been sitting nearby were standing in the aisle now, concerned for the distraught woman. They had had their backs turned when the saloon owner had touched her, and did not notice his startled expression or the way he was holding his hand. "My dear, you are obviously lost," the kind wife said. "And though it is no dishonor to ask strangers for help, I fully understand your hesitance sitting with two strange men."

The husband leaned in, smiling at the former miner and the saloon owner. "No offense, gentlemen, you understand," he smiled. "My wife speaks only for the gentle sensibilities of the fairer among us."

"None taken," said the red-faced ex-miner, who was trying to figure out what to make of the suddenly silenced saloon owner.

The woman turned to the couple, tears gathering, threatening to spill down her pretty face. "Please, answer me. You must know. Has he boarded this train? Is he here? I am afraid that he is here!" Each question was louder than the last, and by the time she voiced her last, it was a shout.

"Well, my goodness," the now-exasperated wife clucked. "I'm sure I have no idea who you're talking about, young lady!" She grabbed her husband by the sleeve and went to turn around but found that she was stuck, hemmed in by several other curious passengers.

Gathered in to see what the fuss was about, the small crowd was full of questions: "What's her problem?" "Something about a guy on the train." "There's someone here she's running from?" "Wants to hurt her." And so it went.

With each muttered statement, the woman grew more visibly distressed. "Yes! Yes!" she was shouting now. "He wants to hurt me! He wants me dead! There is no reasoning with him, and he will never let me go! I must get away! Someone please! Help me!"

The woman had lost herself to panic now. She was shouting a string of frantic pleas. He was almost on her, now, she screamed. "I can feel him! He is close! He is here! He is here!" She tried to get up from her seat, but once she was on her feet, her eyes rolled back and, on the brink of fainting, she collapsed back into her seat.

There were shouts in the confused crowd. "Who's after her?!" "What's this woman on about?!" "Crazy. She's gone crazy! Plumb loco!" A number of the passengers pushed forward to get a closer look, and the effect of the mass pressing toward her made the woman worse.

"Get away from me!" she screeched. "He's going to kill me!"

The ex-miner stood up then, planting himself between the crowd and the hysterical woman. "You heard the lady," he boomed, grateful that he was finally given an opportunity to act, to show his mettle. This woman wanted these people away from her. It was a simple request, something he could understand in all this confusion. Making an effort to ignore the disturbing sight of the saloon owner, who was still staring agape at the woman, he pushed the crowd back, stating that she was obviously confused and needed space.

Yet almost as soon as the crowd backed up, the woman got to her feet and slid by the young man. "I must leave. He is almost here!" she cried as she went.

"Miss!" the young man hollered, reaching out to grab her as she passed. However, the moment his fingers closed around her arm, an ice-cold shock stung his hand, jolted up his arm and seized his chest. Her arm was so cold that it burned. The former miner let out a yelp and collapsed into his seat next to the saloon owner, who was still clutching his own hand in shock.

The sight of the big man falling silenced the crowd, but the woman was oblivious to it, frantically looking about, needing to escape somewhere, but not knowing where. This silence was broken by the sound of the car door sliding open. Everyone turned to see the train conductor stroll into the passenger car. Upon seeing the scene before him, he froze in disbelief. "Impossible," he breathed. "Essie? Essie Mentzer? How can it be? You're dead. You died."

With these words, the young woman let out a shriek. It was a terrible sound, a cry of ineffable grief and horror, which a good number of the people in that passenger car would spend many years trying to forget. And then, in the next moment, she was gone. There was a collective gasp as the beautiful woman who had caused so much commotion vanished right before their eyes, blinking out of sight as quickly and suddenly as a light going out. So went the first sighting of the ghost of Essie Mentzer, who would continue to ride the Rio Grande Southern line out of Telluride for years to come.

Hers was a tragic story. Essie was a pretty woman from Chicago who, by everyone's estimation, had married well when she wed a young physician named O.F. Mentzer. Unfortunately for young Essie, Dr. Mentzer was not as fine a catch as his credentials suggested. Charming as he appeared among friends and acquaintances in Chicago society, the doctor had a dark side that he kept to himself.

Essie had become uneasy about her husband's drinking early on in their marriage. When he took to drink, he tended to become boorish and abusive. The behavior got worse with time. Early on, he limited his abuse to rude comments about her and her family. Less than one year later, he was regularly drunk beyond all reason, sauntering around the house half-clothed with a straight razor in one hand and a pistol in the other, making all sorts of brutal demands of his poor wife.

It only got worse when the doctor began writing double prescriptions, one prescription for his patient and one for himself. Now routinely under the influence of myriad medications, his violent tendencies went wild. More than once, his frothing fits of rage sent Essie screaming from her house. It was not uncommon for neighbors to spy Dr. Mentzer close behind his horror-struck wife, completely naked and brandishing a fork, candleholder or some other improvised weapon. The day he came at her with an ax, however, was the day that Essie decided enough was enough. Social conventions be damned; she would gladly take the shame of divorce over another day with her horrific husband.

But Dr. Mentzer took off before the divorce papers could be signed. He wrote Essie a letter, telling her that he was deeply ashamed of his behavior and that he was going out west to reform himself. "It is out on the frontier," he wrote, "where a man can remake himself in an image that is as good and as pure as the wild beauty of that great land. I hope one day to be worthy of you again." And with these words, Dr. Mentzer departed for Telluride, hoping to "remake himself" in the grand image of the Rockies. It was an honorable intention. Unfortunately for Essie, she took it to heart.

After a less than a month apart, Essie went to Telluride to join her reformed (she thought) husband. It did not take her long to discover that, rather than remake him into a nobler version of himself, the frontier had set free the depraved beast within. His month in Telluride had made him into a monster.

To Essie's young eyes, the devil inside was not readily visible. Indeed, when he met her at the train station, he was as handsome and clear-eyed as he had been when she first met him. She went back to his home sure that she had back the man she married. Little did she know how wrong she was.

The frontier did not drive the insanity from Dr. Mentzer's soul, it only gave it a keener edge. Where he had once been wont to consume every drug in his path and go on binges of stupid and senseless violence, in Telluride he learned to become much more careful in the way he practiced his evil. Left alone with his thoughts in that San Juan town, he became aware of and learned to accept his two-faced nature. He was a literal Dr. Jekyll and Mr. Hyde, who, in the end, chose to present the charming Dr. Jekyll side of his character in order to satiate the psychotic urges of his Mr. Hyde.

Essie was not in Telluride for long when she discovered this fracture in her husband's personality. In public, he had never been so polished. Dressed immaculately without a flaw in his cool manners, he also made sure that Essie enjoyed every luxury a woman could want, a fact that she was encouraged to show off. Truthfully, Essie herself rather enjoyed strutting up and down the streets of Telluride on her handsome husband's arm, sporting clothing and jewelry most of the women there could only dream about. But behind closed doors, it was a different picture altogether.

He had ceased being so brutish and out of control in his expressions of violence, but they had become all the more terrifying for this newfound deliberation. In Chicago, it was his habit to explode in uncontrolled fits; in Telluride, he was controlled, calculated and far more perverse. His wickedness revealed itself slowly, with small, deliberate acts of maliciousness. By the time Essie grasped the direness of her husband's psychosis, she felt powerless to act. Not only was her family too far away to protect her, but there was also the question of propriety. In those days, for a woman to leave her husband once was bad enough, but to leave him twice? That would be a scandal she would never be able to live down.

It is impossible to know how badly Essie suffered before her husband's perversity began to reveal itself in town—a drunken rant here, a chilling threat there. More and more, he was being spotted drunk in the middle of the day. Stories began circulating that he had begun making good use of his medicinal store. There were whispers that former female patients complained of suspected "improprieties" in his clinic.

In the midst of this, in early October 1898, Essie's brother, Will Monroe, arrived in Telluride with his wife to visit his sister. It is likely that Essie had not informed her family of her husband's behavior, as Will and his wife ended up staying at the Mentzer home, in which the doctor made sure they were entertained in grand fashion. In the short time the couple was there, they were given no reason to believe anything was wrong—until, that is, it was too late.

On the evening of October 7, the two couples were up late, talking about business prospects in Colorado over drinks. Well, this was what Will and Dr. Mentzer were talking about. Will's wife, however, could see how anxious Essie was. How she cast a nervous, sidelong glance every time her husband poured himself another glass of scotch. The way she began to fidget whenever the doctor left the room "to administer to something," as he put it, in his bedroom. By this time Will was quite drunk, but his wife saw the way Dr. Mentzer was whenever he returned from his "administrations." His eyes were glassy, and his speech was slurred.

"The doctor, he really seems to have cleaned up his act, hasn't he, dear?" an inebriated Will Monroe said to his wife that night as they were getting ready for bed. "And poor Essie seems so happy now, wouldn't you say?"

His wife was just about to snort her response when a scream sounded from downstairs in the parlor, where they had just left Essie and Dr. Mentzer. "Help me!" It was Essie's voice. "He's going to kill me!"

Will Munroe flew down the stairs and threw open the parlor door. There he stood stunned before a horrific sight. In the room where, just minutes ago, he had shaken Dr. Mentzer's hand and kissed Essie on the cheek, his brother-in-law was holding a pistol in his upraised hand, having just cracked the barrel across Essie's head.

"By God, Mentzer! What the devil do you think you're doing?!" But the doctor was beyond reason. Leering at Munroe through bloodshot eyes, he pulled Essie close, put the gun to her head and pulled the trigger. Essie died on her feet, pleading for her brother to save her.

Before she fell to the floor Munroe had closed his hands around her killer's throat, yanking the pistol from his hands and beating the drugged up doctor until his knuckles bled, until he had no more strength, until there were no more bones in Dr. Mentzer's body to break. But it did not help his sister, who lay bloody on her parlor floor, her eyes locked in her last expression—eternal pleading.

It was this same pleading look that the passengers on the Rio Grande Southern would see a few weeks later when she appeared on the train out of Telluride, trying to get out of town about a month too late. When she vanished after the conductor recognized her, it was said that her spirit was making the trip back to Chicago, where her body was buried. The more optimistic storytellers like to end the tale with how the train took her all the way home, and the ghost of young Essie was able to rest in peace.

Unfortunately though, this was not the last time the panic-stricken apparition was spotted on the night train out of Colorado. Indeed, for as long as the Rio Grande Southern connected Telluride to the outside world, the ghost of Essie Mentzer was known to ride it—always at night, always with the same mortal desperation.

And yet her tragedy, in life as well as in death, is that she was never able to make it away. It was always the same story. With every successive mile, she grew more anxious, feeling the presence of her homicidal husband get stronger and stronger. She always vanished the moment someone on the train recognized her and called her by name. If that didn't happen before she was 10 miles out of town, she would just vanish on her own, unable to deal with the dread of her unseen husband's approach any longer. Those 10 miles were as far out of Telluride as Essie Mentzer was ever able to get.

Other Spirits on the San Juan Rails

Essie Mentzer was not the only spirit to haunt the Rio Grande Southern running through the San Juan range in southwest Colorado. There is no shortage of supernatural legends originating from the famous narrow-gauge track that wound its treacherous way through the gorges and mountainsides of this most impassable part of the state. Its construction alone proved to be quite the feat, during which work crews and engineers, demonstrating unearthly determination, blasted a path through the mountains. Between 1890 and 1891, the rocky peaks and steep valleys resounded with the echoes of railway men doing their next-to-impossible work.

And many perished while laying the tracks up the steep grades, over the soaring bridges or through the tunnels. Dynamite blasts, exposure to the elements, avalanches, overwork—the tale of the railway is a chronicle of death and danger, peopled by wage earners who were willing to risk their lives for a buck. And the deaths did not stop when the railway was completed.

The Rio Grande Southern through the San Juan Mountains was one of the scariest lines to ride. Even disregarding the steep switchbacks, the narrow bridges over seemingly bottomless gorges and the precipice-lined corners, the forces of nature appeared set on confounding this man-made construction. There were regular avalanches and blizzards in winter and rockslides and flash floods in spring. Deep in the San Juan, there was no small number of men who lost their lives along this perilous way. And with the San Juan dead came the San Juan ghosts.

Trains tracks are actually well-known sites for hauntings. All across the country there are ghostly hobos riding the trains they knew while they were alive. There are those who were killed by oncoming traffic, those who died on trains, and those, like Essie Mentzer, desperately trying to get away from a place. There are even phantom trains, well-loved locomotives speeding over long-discontinued lines, silent and glimmering in the night. The treacherous tracks through the San Juan were plagued by all manner of such phenomena.

The earliest stories date back to the first trains, in the early 1890s, shortly after the Rio Grande Southern line was opened. Of them, the most repeated is the tale of the swinging light on the way to Durango. Appearing numerous times to locomotive engineers when a train pulled into the valleys along the Delores River, the oscillating light proved itself, time and again, as a railway man's best friend.

A typical telling of the story has an engineer peering watchfully into the darkness as his iron horse chugs south through the San Juan. Usually, the engineer ignores the light at the first sighting. It is small, after all, a tiny circle swinging back and forth just beyond the locomotive light, and it barely lasts—the engineer who witnesses it just starts thinking of the possibility that someone ahead is swinging a signal light when it blinks out of sight.

When it appears again, usually just a few minutes later, the alert engineer takes it far more seriously. It seems a little bit closer now, waving a bit quicker; there is a sense of urgency. At this point, the engineer grabs his fireman or his brakeman to get a second opinion, but the moment the coworker shows up at the engineer's side, the light vanishes again. The engineer is left alone again, now peering anxiously ahead, feeling increasingly uneasy about the situation.

The third time the light appears, he does not hesitate and whistles for the brakeman to stop. The screeching train hasn't reached a full stop when the engineer jumps down and runs ahead, lantern held high, to take a look and see what is ahead. He is hoping that there is indeed something there so that he doesn't look like a fool to his crew. There is never anyone there. No sight of a swinging lantern and nothing to indicate that anyone had ever been there. But then, ahead on the tracks, the narrowly averted disaster becomes visible; there has been a rockslide, and boulders are strewn across the tracks. If the engineer had not stopped on account of the light, there would have surely been a collision.

There are always variations to these sightings of the swinging light, but they are generally the same: an incredulous engineer spots the mysterious signal light; he ignores it once or twice, maybe three times, but he eventually decides to stop the train; he always makes the discovery, then, that if he had not stopped, his train may very well have been wrecked.

The prevailing theory behind these phantom lights is that they are being wielded by the ghosts of railway men who died on that stretch of track. They are ghostly sentinels wielding their signal lanterns to warn their coworkers of imminent danger, perhaps as a show of workers' solidarity surviving beyond the grave. It was the 19th century, after all, a time when labor unions were some of the most important organizations in society. If it seems implausible now, one need read only a bit about the great Pullman strike to get an idea of how strongly railway men felt about one another. Who knows? Perhaps their ghosts were looking out for their still-living associates.

Other tales revolving around the San Juan tracks told of train employees who so loved their jobs that they continued to do them after they had passed. Apparitions of dead conductors, pale as bone, silent as the grave and semi-transparent to boot, wandered up and down the aisles of certain trains, checking the tickets of disconcerted passengers. There were also accounts from engineers who, while piloting their trains through the darkness, were suddenly seized by the feeling that something was very wrong. Looking over, they would discover the cause. There, standing right next to them would be another engineer, keenly staring into the darkness ahead, hand closed around the throttle—alert, as any good engine driver ought to be. The ghostly engineer would be there one instant and gone the next, leaving startled engineers wondering if they were losing their minds.

As miserable and scared as the spirit of Essie Mentzer was, at least it can be said that she was not alone. Indeed, there were a good number of stories about phantom passengers that continued to ride the rails after they had passed. Unlike the unhappy Essie, the ghost of Isidor Henschel never did anything to draw attention to himself. He simply appeared on the train from Rico to Ophir just when the locomotive began chugging up the ascent to Lizard Head Pass. His manifestation was always the same: a young man, looking as real and alive as anyone else, sitting at a window seat, wearing the crisp Navy uniform he had been buried in. Most times, he appeared so gradually that people did not even notice he was there. Then, just as quietly, he would fade out of sight when the train approached Rice Spur.

Isidor's death, however, was not nearly as dignified as his ghostly manifestation might suggest. A hobo hitching a ride in one of the freight cars, aiming to get to Ophir on the cheap, he was killed in a train crash in 1901. Disaster struck at Rice Spur, soon after the train peaked Lizard Head Pass. Unfortunately for Isidor, not enough of the train had cleared Lizard Head; when it stopped to pick up a load of lumber, it began to slide backward. All the way down the side of the mountain he flew, along with the freight cars full of lumber. Railway men found him later as they were sifting through the wreckage, crushed to death amid a pile of wood.

On the same line from Rico to Ophir, the ghost of the tragically accident prone James McDonald is also said to appear, sitting blankly in passenger cars for a few moments before vanishing suddenly right in front of startled passengers. A wounded miner who had just been released from several months of convalescence in a Rico hospital, James McDonald was cleared to go on a bright morning in March 1892. He would die a gruesome and terrible death that very same day.

It came about on account of one unlucky decision. Almost as soon as he boarded the train to Ophir, McDonald began to get restless. He had just spent a good amount of time bedridden in a hospital, and the last thing he was in the mood for was more sitting still. Deciding to get up and walk around, he soon found himself on his way to the engine room. He had always wanted to get a close look at the way a locomotive worked. And so it was that the luckless McDonald entered the locomotive moments before it went flying off the rail, caught wrong in the tracks at the Glencoe switch. With a screech, a hiss and a crash, the locomotive rolled. Everyone in the engine room was badly scalded by the steam, but McDonald got it worst; he was burned alive under a jet of scorching vapor.

One railway-related death that was nearly as gruesome involved a mysterious, heavily tattooed man who put his neck on the tracks in the Telluride depot. Nothing is known about this man's motivations, but he had long been considered one of the town's more idiosyncratic citizens. After the incident, his apparition was encountered several times by clerks watching over baggage cars out of Telluride. Low, miserable moans coming from one of the baggage compartments alerted these clerks that something was amiss. It was just a matter of swinging open a single door, and a baggage clerk would be traumatized for life.

For there, standing on the other side of the door, was the headless man, his arms and torso bedecked in tattoos of women and religious icons from myriad faiths, holding his own bleeding head aloft with an outstretched arm.

The stories of haunts on the Rio Grande Southern went on and on. It seemed that as long as the mining boom in the San Juan Mountains continued to draw superstitious men and women into that rough region, tales of the walking dead circulated and grew. For reasons unknown, the railway that cut through this region was something of a locus for paranormal activity. But when the mining boom in the San Juan Mountains died, so too did the trains that took people there. The traffic on the railway lines dried up, and one after another, they shut down. The ghostly accounts went with them—for the most part, anyway.

Among certain train aficionados, those rails that wound through the San Juan Mountains are nothing short of legendary. For many, those early locomotives, defying such impossible landscapes and bringing industry to the most inaccessible places in the nation, came to embody the ambition and ability of American enterprise. And they have not been easily forgotten. Indeed, to this day there are some who would say that even though the old locomotives no longer run, something of their *spirit* remains to chug along those high mountain rails.

Spirit? How can a train have a spirit?

Perhaps the people best qualified to answer that question would be those who claim to have seen the silvery apparitions of the old trains racing through the San Juan on long-abandoned tracks, gliding through the gorges or over the passes without a sound, moving faster than any train today. Although there obviously can no longer be fresh encounters with spirits on trains that no longer run, some might say that the trains themselves have become the ghosts—ghosts that continue to haunt the peaks and valleys of the San Juan, through which they once sped with such noise, dirt and grandeur.

4
Native Spirits and Unexplained Phenomenas

The Spirits on Sand Creek

It simply is not possible for Indians to obey or even understand any treaty. I am fully satisfied, gentlemen, that to kill them is the only way we will ever have peace and quiet in Colorado.

—John M. Chivington, September 1864

His name was John M. Chivington, and he was one of Colorado's most celebrated and deplored citizens. A strapping Methodist preacher who saw no contradiction in combining his religious beliefs with violent action, he possessed an unshakeable faith and a willingness to go to any lengths to fight for what he believed in—traits that served him well under the looming shadow of the Civil War.

In many biographies, he began his public career in 1856 as a burly young minister in Missouri, preaching a strident anti-slavery sermon to a congregation largely sympathetic to the Confederate cause. He did not pause when whole rows of parishioners got up and left midway through his service. The next Sunday, after he had been threatened with tarring and feathering if he continued to preach, he showed up with his Bible in one hand and two loaded pistols tucked into his belt. Climbing up to the pulpit, he looked over his hushed congregation, cleared his voice and said: "By the Grace of God and these two revolvers, I'm going to preach here today."

So it was that Chivington, now hailed as the "Fighting Parson," became something of an antebellum celebrity. In 1860 he moved to Denver to serve as the elder of the Methodist Church's Rocky Mountain District. When the Civil War broke out, the governor offered Chivington a commission in the First Colorado Volunteer Regiment, but he refused, famously proclaiming that he would much rather fight than pray. The preacher's feverish look made it clear: he was deadly serious. The governor changed the offer, and Chivington traded his minister's cloth for an officer's uniform.

The biggest battles of the Civil War were fought in the East, but Chivington milked the skirmishes in the West for all the glory they were worth. He won his laurels in the battle of Glorietta Pass, in New Mexico Territory, when he distinguished himself in a number of decisive engagements over the course of the three-day battle.

After the war, Chivington made as much political currency out of his wartime experience as he was able. He became a leading citizen in Denver and was looking to become the Republican candidate for the territory's first Congressional election. A man who had won his popularity based on conflict, Chivington must have recognized he was in need of more conflict to secure his political ambitions.

Lucky for him, it was the mid-1860s, and there was no shortage of conflict in the Colorado Territory. There were the Cheyenne and Arapaho on one side, and the miners on the other. Hostile braves saw the seemingly endless wave of miners flowing into their traditional hunting grounds as nothing less than an invasion, while the recently arrived white populations tended to regard the indigenous peoples as indolent primitives whose fate it was to submit to the white man's ambitions and fall in line with the "civilization" he brought with him.

In fact, that Natives should merely submit to the white man's rule was a fairly mild opinion held by new settlers. Others argued that Native peoples were, by nature, treacherous, inferior and hostile and ought to be exterminated. In that age of widespread fear and unchecked avarice, it was a belief that had much popular support. It was a belief John Chivington shared, and he was all too eager to turn the popular anger at the Cheyenne and Arapaho's upped hostility to his political advantage.

Railing against Colorado's governor for taking an easy stance with the Cheyenne, he denounced all who argued for peaceful negotiation. There was no room for treaties with the Cheyenne and Arapaho, he said, claiming that it was impossible for Native peoples to even understand, much less adhere to, such contracts. When he announced that mass extermination was the answer, he was greeted with more support than most of us today would care to admit. Taking the public reaction as general consent, he went about looking for an opportunity to prove his greatness—or, as it turned out, to propel him to infamy.

Early on the morning of November 29, 1864, Chivington was looking over a Native encampment on the big bend of Sand Creek. There were about 500 souls camped there, mostly Cheyenne and a small number of Arapaho. The majority of them were old men, women and children, people who had no stomach for the fight against the white man. They had rallied to the pacific chief Black Kettle, who was leading his people under a promise of protection from the government of the United States. Chivington would have been able to see the white flag and the American flag flying from Black Kettle's tent as he ordered his soldiers to take position around the settlement.

Chivington also had full knowledge of the status of negotiations with the local tribes, and he knew that Black Kettle's people were flying a flag of truce. But he could find no Cheyenne war parties to fight and still had his eye trained on his political prize. In the face of political expediency, it did not matter in the least that there was hardly a warrior among the settlers. He ordered his soldiers into firing lines and trained his howitzers on the defenseless tepees along the creek.

What followed was one of the most infamous attacks in American military history; Chivington's men attacked with zealous brutality. It began with a heavy barrage of artillery and rifle fire. When the Cheyenne and Arapaho scattered in panic, Chivington's men rushed forward, ready to turn the attack into a massacre. On that November morning on the plains of southeast Colorado, they made a statement—with their sabers, pistols, hatchets, knives and rifles, they carved a testament of human depravity into the annals of American history.

A surviving interpreter in Black Kettle's camp later told of the atrocities that were committed on the elderly, the women and the children who were too weak to run: "They were scalped, their brains knocked out; the men used their knives, ripped open women, clubbed little children, knocked them in the head with their rifle butts, beat their brains out, mutilated their bodies in every sense of the word."

Black Kettle's people fought as best as they were able, but they were hopelessly outnumbered, and there were few among them able to wield a rifle or a hatchet with any skill. Their blood colored Sand Creek that day. Nine of Chivington's men were killed in the fighting, while anywhere between 200 and 400 Cheyenne and Arapaho died at the hands of battle-crazed, bloodthirsty Colorado volunteers.

Chivington's men came away from the massacre with appalling trophies—scalps, dismembered heads, fingers and organs of their victims—held high. In Denver, Chivington announced they had won a major battle against hostile Cheyenne, and he and his men were promptly celebrated in the press, hailed as heroes, great men returning from a victory against the savages of the plains.

In the end, Chivington's glory did not last. The following weeks saw traumatized soldiers coming forward with the true story of what had occurred. An investigation followed, and Chivington was publicly disgraced. A good many citizens in the Colorado Territory had little love for the Native peoples, but most agreed that Chivington had gone too far. Although the prevailing attitude against the Natives allowed him to escape a court martial, he would never realize his political aspirations and ended up dying in obscurity in some 30 years later.

But what happened at Sand Creek lived on. Legends of the goings-on there began soon after the dust settled on that November morning. Lone buffalo hunters camping near the big bend of Sand Creek would wake in the morning to find themselves a stone's throw from a massive Cheyenne settlement. The climate of the times was such that these men would shoot up from their sleeping rolls and go straight for their rifles. Yet even before they had their hands on their guns, they unfailingly stopped, noticing that no sound, not even a whisper, rose from the encampment—noticing as well that none of the Cheyenne were moving, but were standing by their tepees, men, women and children, as still as the landscape, all staring out on the stark world around them with looks of blank accusation.

There has been significant variation regarding what happens next. Some men have turned and fled, heading straight for the nearest outpost, Fort Lyon, where they reported the presence of hundreds of Cheyenne camped at the big bend in the creek. At first, these testimonies resulted in scouts being sent out to investigate, but the reports always came back the same: not a soul, Cheyenne or otherwise, was anywhere near Sand Creek.

Other witnesses stuck around long enough to see the disappearing act themselves. These dumbfounded drifters, paralyzed by the bizarre sight, could only stare as the mute band of Cheyenne wavered and then blinked out of sight right before their eyes. One moment, there was the deathly congregation, and the next, nothing but the creek, the sky and the wide-open prairie.

Wanderers through the region spoke of other phenomena through the latter decades of the 19th century. There were repeated stories of powerful voices heard near the creek, innumerable voices suddenly chanting, rising and then falling mute, lost just as suddenly as they came in the gusting prairie wind. Sometimes the chanting was accompanied by the sight of countless tepees, a vision that would remain no longer than the voices, suddenly appearing and then disappearing just as quickly.

There were also those who never actually saw or heard anything on that bloodied ground, but were deeply affected by the *feeling* there. This feeling, alternately described as a cold chill, an inexplicable sense of foreboding or else an unnerving feeling of being watched by hundreds of invisible faces, had a way of keeping many people away from the site of the massacre. Once travelers felt the mortal cold on the banks of Sand Creek, they were not likely to return any time soon.

The years have brought no small number of rumors and suppositions—if not visible apparitions or audible phenomena, then less tangible, sensory impressions— undeniable adrenaline rushes occurring for no apparent reason or the feeling some visitors got that they were in immediate danger, though there was no threat visible. Others arriving at the bend in the creek claimed to have heard dogs barking and children shouting when neither dogs nor children were present. To this very day, bizarre accounts continue to circulate. As recently as 1997, individuals participating in archeological digs in the region went away speaking of being overcome by a nearly over-whelming sense of sadness.

The site of the massacre has come to occupy a promi-nent place in the spiritual landscape of the Cheyenne. It is the burial ground that never was, a still-living symbol of the atrocities of the 19th century. Among the Cheyenne there is a sense of violent disruption, grief and betrayal on this stretch of prairie. The spirits there not only haunt the bloodied banks of Sand Creek, but also the Cheyenne culture, identity and politics. Wherever the Cheyenne are, there too are the spirits of Sand Creek.

The Serpent Under
the Mountain

They came at night, black figures, silent as shadows, passing into the settlements of those Ute, Cheyenne or Arapaho who had unknowingly camped too close to their mountainous dwelling places. Most of the time, they came and went without anyone knowing. Not until first light would it be known, when the settlement was woken by an anguished wail from one of the families. Someone was gone. One of the revered elderly, or else one of the adored infants—gone forever, abducted in their sleep to face a terrible fate. They belonged, now, to the Snake People.

Readers would be hard pressed to find any record of them in anthropological studies or historical monographs. No remains have ever been found in the alpine landscapes they have been said to inhabit. It cannot really be said that they have been forgotten, per se, as most academics studying the Native clans of the Rocky Mountains would likely insist that they never even existed.

And yet the legend is there, little more than a sidebar in the mythos of the Rocky Mountains—the dreaded Snake People, elusive and deadly, their hidden settlements dotted throughout Colorado and Montana in the mountains' highest reaches. It is important that they not be mistaken for the Shoshone—or Snake Nation—who occupied much of the land in the Great Basin. There is no relation whatsoever. The Snake People were all but invisible, having never warred with a neighboring tribe, never traded a single hide, never rustled a horse and never drawn from the pipe with any elder from any other tribe.

The terrible people from the highlands cared not for any of these things. Their sole purpose was to tend to their serpents. Inhabitants of a sparse, mountainous environment that did not allow for large settlements, the dark tribe's warriors went about in small groups, ruthlessly preying on neighboring tribes for their very young and their very old. It was said that each clan took care of one enormous viper. These monstrous serpents were living totems, which were kept well fed by a steady stream of involuntary sacrifices. It was the constant pursuit of these sacrifices that kept the Snake People busy, creeping into tribal settlements when they needed a living person for their gruesome rites.

The Natives closest to the rocky summits had the most trouble. No one had ever stumbled on one of the Snake People's settlements and lived to tell about it, so it was impossible to say where they were. The fact that they were able to appear suddenly in the middle of a settlement and then vanish again without leaving a trace of their passing led some to believe that they traveled by tunnels dug deep under the mountains. It was up through these tunnels they came, sneaking into the midst of a sleeping camp and then vanishing with their victims.

Over time, there was more than one wakeful brave who caught sight of the shadows darting through his camp. And more than once, settlements were woken by fierce war cries as braves rushed to stop these predatory interlopers. The warning would resound through the settlement. "The Snake People! They are here! Check for your young! Check for your old!"

The aftermath was always the same. After the last hatchet was swung and the last rifle was fired, the dark scene revealed dozens of dead warriors—not one of them numbering among their assailants. In all the years they terrorized the Rockies, no one was ever known to have struck down one of the Snake People. Those who fought them and lived told of how they might as well have been fighting nothing more than shadows—shadows that bore sharp hatchets and hard knives, shadows that darted like serpents and struck with otherworldly strength. The men who faced them and lived told the stories that made them into devils. They were warriors who fought with the darkest magic on their side—untouchable, invincible.

There were times when the serpentine tribe came down from the mountains with nothing more than death and terror in mind. They descended, then, alongside the enormous serpents they guarded. The warriors watched over the sleeping camp as the massive snakes slithered into a tribe's horse pens. Their attacks were silent and lethal. A dart and a flash and a horse would fall, twitching to death as the venom spread. And another, and another, until every one of the prized beasts were killed.

As with the abductions, these slaughters usually went undetected, completely silent, only to be discovered the next morning. And those who did look upon these massive vipers doing their grisly work would never be able to forget—the two enormous serpent eyes staring from the darkness; the chilling size of the body; the fanged mouth, large enough to fit around a horse's neck.

And yet, as much of a menace as the Snake People were to tribes situated around the Rockies, they were nothing compared to the massive slaughter and displacement that European settlers brought with them. The problems with the Snake People took a back seat when miners, ranchers and farmers began flooding into the region. And so it was that as the Natives indigenous to the Rocky Mountains faced the end of their ways, the tales of the Snake People were largely forgotten.

Nevertheless, if some accounts are to be trusted, it seems as though the predatory serpent worshippers might not have suffered the same fate as their quarry. For it wasn't long after Colorado was settled that incredible stories about enormous serpents and mysterious shadows in the night began emerging from small pockets of settlers in and around the Rockies. It has been said that as the white man took over all the inhabitable land, the Snake People climbed higher and burrowed deeper into the mountains, avoiding detection as they had before. And then over time, they began preying on the white settlers the way they had the Native tribes before them.

Early miners, ranchers and farmers living near the mountains would mysteriously lose their babies and their elderly in the middle of the night. Ranchers woke in the morning to find scores of their cattle dead—throats torn open, filled with enough venom to kill an elephant. Settlers lost cattle, horses, mules and pigs. Those unfortunate few that laid eyes on the perpetrators of these crimes were scarred for life. Stories of darting shadows and enormous serpents began to circulate among terrified frontiersmen.

Might those 19th century Natives confined to reservations have heard these rumors? Maybe they found themselves sympathetic to their former enemies, hoping, perhaps, that the evil in the mountains would drive the white settlers away. This did not happen. Instead, it seemed as though the serpent worshippers were retreating into their mountains as the years passed, emerging from their underground lairs less and less. By the end of the 1800s, run-ins with the mysterious mountain-dwellers were rare.

But this isn't to say that they ceased all together. In his book, *Ghosts of the Old West*, Earl Murray narrates his account of a young man who spotted a gigantic snake one night in the summer of 1982. According to Murray, this man, an Apache Indian going by the pseudonym "Mahlan," was driving to his sister's home somewhere in the central Rockies when he saw the beast. Only a few miles from his sister's home, Mahlan had gotten out of his car to open a gate barring the road when a stifling odor filled the air; Mahlan recognized the smell of a pit viper. The snake appeared just after he got back in his car—two narrow, yellow eyes sitting about three feet apart in a head he couldn't make out clearly in the darkness. Suddenly filled with terror, Mahlan was only able to stare at the creature in fear, convinced that these would be his final moments. And then the snake turned and slithered away, vanishing into the night. Mahlan drove to his sister's ranch as fast as his car would take him.

Telling her about his experience on the road later that night, Mahlan was surprised to learn that his sister and brother-in-law's cattle had been dying for quite some time, their poisoned carcasses turning up along the river's edge. It was then that Mahlan's sister told him about the Snake People and how she had seen them late at night, their dark silhouettes darting about the compound.

It seems, then, that the old Native legend may still persist, though not with the same vehemence that it once had. Had there ever actually been a Snake People? Underground tunnels in the Rockies? Invincible, wraith-like warriors? Giant serpents in the mountains? Plain curiosity might impel us to find answers, but simple wisdom might advise us to just accept that we may never know. Given how integral terror and death are to the narrative, perhaps it is enough to be thankful that the legend does not circulate they way it once did, and be hopeful that it remains that way.

What Was Buried in Las Animas

In the winter of 1870, a farmer named Juan Vasquez was out on his land, digging a foundation for a house, when he hit something hard with the tip of his shovel. Harder, that is, than the tough Las Animas dirt he'd been breaking throughout the day—hard enough to make him stop, wipe the sweat from his brow and curse. "¡Maldita sea!" Had he hit bedrock? If he wasn't able to dig further, he would have to quit and start again somewhere else—an entire day of work wasted.

He dug around the thing he had struck, and found that the earth yielded around the hard object he had discovered. It was small. He would be able to dig around it. A few minutes later, he was able to make out a smooth, spherical object jutting from the ground, then a hollow in the surface, another hollow, a ridge between the two hollows. *Could it be?* He dug a little further and confirmed his suspicion. He had just unearthed a human skull.

And not just any human skull. He gasped when he withdrew it from the earth. The skull was enormous, easily twice the normal size. This man or woman had to have been freakishly big—a giant. Vasquez stood agape, staring in disbelief, trying to comprehend the magnitude of his discovery. But he would not have much time; the skull remained intact for only a few minutes before it began to break apart in his hands, crumbling to dust and broken fragments.

He reached down and grabbed his shovel, moving quickly, with urgency. If there was a skull, there would be other bones—more evidence of the incredible find he had unearthed. Indeed, he might even be standing on a burial ground. Vasquez dug feverishly, possessed by the prospect of other giant-sized skulls beneath his feet. And there were. Several.

He unearthed several entire skeletons, the brittle remains of some gigantic subspecies of humanity unrecorded by science or history, here in the sprawling county of Las Animas. *A race of giants!* Vasquez was in the thrall of fresh discovery. His imagination took over. He saw a time when the country was home to a giant people. They would have to rewrite history. And he would be famous for it. He pictured it in his mind: *Juan Vasquez: the man who discovered the race of giants on his land.* Or better yet, perhaps these giants buried their treasures with them? Maybe with the next jab of his shovel, he would hit a box instead of bones. And what if inside this box, there was…

No. Juan Vasquez was a practical man, not given to such delusional fits. In the end, it was a good thing he was blessed with such a grounded disposition. For not only was there no treasure to be found, but the skeletons themselves did not last. Like the first skull he pulled from the earth, the bones began to crumble soon after they were laid down on the ground. Skulls dissolved into mounds of bone chips, rib cages collapsed into the dirt, femurs became splinters. By the end of the day, all Vasquez had to show for his work was a gaping hole in the earth and a few wheelbarrows of bone dust.

But that was not the end of the story. Bransford Ranch lay about half a mile east of Vasquez's property. Mr. Bransford ran a tight operation with the help of his son, a strapping 20-year-old who was raised on the frontier. On the night of the same day that Vasquez made his discovery, strange forces came to visit Bransford Ranch.

Bransford's son, having woken from a fitful dream, was on his way to the outhouse when a figure appeared before him. It was a man, a Native of a tribe that young Bransford did not recognize. The man was obviously of some prominence in his tribe, standing tall and broad, with a stern countenance. His skin looked a bit too pale for any Native that Bransford had seen, and he was dressed in brilliant white clothing that shone, luminescent, in the darkened doorway. Young Bransford froze, unable to register the impossible sight before him. It was only when the figure in white moved, turning and beckoning the young rancher to follow, that he snapped out of his paralysis. Turning and running back into the house, he woke one of his father's ranch hands and shouted at the man to follow him. When they returned to the doorway, there was no one there.

The ranch boss, Mr. Bransford himself, slept soundly through the racket his son was making but ended up waking up later, in the small hours of the morning, to the sound of tapping on his door. Upon waking, the first thought that came to Bransford was a question: *Where are my dogs?* The ranch boss owned a number of four-legged guards that were fiercely protective of the ground around the house. They would have never allowed someone to get close enough to knock at his door at this hour, at least not without raising an unholy ruckus. Yet there Bransford was, lying in bed, wondering who the hell could be knocking at his door in the middle of the night.

The rancher pulled himself out of bed. "Who is it?" he growled, picking up his six-shooter off his night table. When there was no answer, he slowly cocked the hammer of his pistol and approached the door. The tapping continued right up until he grabbed the handle and swung the door open, only to find that there was nobody there. He stepped outside and looked around—nothing.

And yet the moment he was back in bed the tapping started again, this time accompanied by a scraping on his ceiling. Time and again he rushed out to catch a glimpse of whatever was tormenting him, but he was never able to catch the culprit. His dogs were just as puzzled as he was, watching their master quizzically as he repeatedly burst from his house, gun drawn, looking around frantically in the darkness.

That night proved to be just the beginning of the bizarre events at Bransford Ranch, so bizarre that they would eventually attract local attention. A report of the goings-on in the out-of-the-way ranch some 20 miles southeast of Trinidad was printed in the December 20, 1870 issue of *The Rocky Mountain News*. By then, a full-fledged supernatural investigation was in effect.

Supernatural investigations are interesting affairs. The notion of applying scientific principles to the research and study of supernatural phenomena originated—and culminated—in the late 19th century, based on a belief that rational and/or psychic research in purportedly haunted sites might reveal certain truths about the afterlife. Unfortunately, so many of these investigations, then, as well as today, ended up yielding very few explanations, while creating a mess of controversy about proper methods and false reporting; then, as well as today, supernatural investigation remained on the dubious fringes of scientific research.

Nevertheless, according to *The Rocky Mountain News*, the investigators at Bransford Ranch were not disappointed with the phenomena they experienced. They did not spot the man in white, nor did they make any record of the scratching sounds on the door and ceiling of Mr. Bransford's room. They did, however, observe two other occurrences that suggested things were not right at the Las Animas ranch.

The thing with the fireplace happened during the team's first night at the ranch. The investigators were sitting around the fire, planning what they were going to do the next day, when movement in the fireplace grabbed their attention.

There in the hearth, two flaming logs had come to life. Suddenly jolting up onto their ends, the two logs began to circle each other, sparking and popping as they went. A stunned silence reigned among the investigators as the logs twirled for a few more seconds before a resounding "pop" startled them from their trance and sent the two pieces of wood shooting straight up the chimney.

Outside the ranch house, the two flaming logs rocketed from the chimney, arced through the night sky and landed on the ground roughly 30 yards away. Moments later, the front door of the house flew open and the investigators set about scurrying through the darkness, lanterns aloft, looking for the two still-glowing logs. It was not long before they found them.

What then followed was scientific method at its finest. They observed the logs for any anomalies, tested for consistency, looked for peculiar markings and sketched the way the logs were lying on the ground.

Did they emit heat? Yes.

Did they respond when spoken to? No.

Was there anything at all that differentiated them from normal pieces of flaming wood, anything that could offer a ready explanation for what just occurred? Unfortunately not. They were painfully typical pieces of wood.

The next day, however, the investigators were tempted to draw some connection with what had occurred in the fireplace and what was going on in Bransford's garden. The two stone mounds had been there when Bransford set up his ranch. The rancher chose not to touch them when he was building his home. For reasons he could never explain, he had always felt slightly uneasy about the two piles of small boulders. There was something about them, he said, that struck him as plain strange, and he thought it best to just leave them undisturbed.

His hunch turned out to be right on. For shortly after the night that the mysterious man in white appeared at the door, one of the mounds began to emit two continuous plumes of dark black smoke. Although he himself refused to touch it, he gave the investigators permission to do whatever they wanted.

The following are the words of one of the investigators, as quoted in the December 20, 1870 issue of *The Rocky Mountain News*:

> On the garden of Mr. Bransford are two piles or mounds of stone. Through one of these mounds issue constantly two small columns of smoke, apparently caused by the burning of wood. Furthermore, the ground for 50 feet in the neighborhood sounds hollow and gives one the feeling as if walking on the deck of a ship.

Smoke issuing from the ground that was "apparently caused by the burning of wood"? The sense that the ground around the piles of stone was hollow, like "walking on the deck of a ship"? Incredible as these observations seem, they somehow made it into a contemporary paper. Unfortunately, no solid evidence concerning the cause of the smoking mounds or hollow earth was found.

The team poked through the stones but discovered nothing. They excavated around the smoking mound, digging as deep as 10 feet in the hopes of finding some sort of explanation, but again, their efforts turned up no answers. Despite the feeling that the ground was somehow hollow, they found they were digging through solid earth. There were no underground caverns, not even any notable change in the consistency of the dirt they labored through.

The one thing they did find, and that only after they had excavated 10 feet under, was a type of stone that, according to established archeological study, had once been used by certain Native groups to grind grain. And thus their investigation was concluded, without any satisfactory answers to the question of what, exactly, was going on at Bransford Ranch.

When the story of what was happening at the Las Animas ranch spread through the region, corroborating accounts emerged. There was the testimony of a Mexican girl who lived about two miles from the ranch and who also saw a man in shining white garments. She claimed she saw him walking slowly past her home late in the night, on the same evening that Bransford's son ran into the figure in the doorway.

And then there was Juan Vasquez and his bag of bone chips. Struck by the timing of all these bizarre incidents, he decided to speak up about the skeletons he had unearthed. Taking with him the bone that had deteriorated least, the brittle remnant of a giant femur, he made a trip to Trinidad, offering up the femur to one Dr. Besohar, thinking the man of science might have some answers— or, at the very least, some suggestions.

After studying the femur carefully, the doctor did not hesitate in offering his professional opinion: the femur fragment was indeed much larger than anything that would be found on *Homo sapiens*. But if Vasquez was hoping that his discovery would make him famous, Dr. Besohar was not so ambitious, and the question of the giant bones never went further than his office.

So concludes the account of what went on in this corner of Colorado so many years ago. Bransford Ranch is no longer there, and there has been no further mention of a smoking pile of rocks, a man dressed in glowing white garments or any more discoveries of giant skeletons—in short, nothing that contemporary supernatural investigators would be able to sink their teeth into. And so goes another unsolved paranormal mystery, long forgotten in the vast county of Las Animas.

Lights on the Prairie

They appeared on the flatlands in the southeastern part of the state. The first sodbusters of Las Animas and Baca counties talked about them, usually in whispers, on those rare occasions when the far-flung homesteading families got together for socials. "You seen any lately?" one grim-faced frontier wife would whisper to another when there were no children close enough to hear.

"Sure did. Bunch of 'em woke me and the kids up in the middle of the night, week before last. Not the husband, though—kept snoring away. Man could sleep through a buffalo stampede."

Of course, they also woke many exhausted frontier men, who stared in wonder or terror through the holes in their sod walls. It was the middle of the night, but out there on the big, lonesome prairie were lights. Sometimes they were distant points, clearly defined circles moving over the horizon. But sometimes they were close, dazzling spotlights that hurt to look at, sharp white lights that lit up the dingy interiors of those early homesteaders' abodes.

Today, it is impossible to account for the wide variety of reactions to and explanations of this phenomenon. The easiest to imagine would be the religious one. It was the 19th century, and these families were about as isolated as human beings could be. Surely such mysterious and unnatural occurrences would turn the more religious to the ultimate explanation for all unknowns: God.

Depending on a settler's disposition and the state of his or her conscience, the lights could be a horrific harbinger of vengeance, or perhaps a wondrous demonstration of divine glory. Given the typical homesteader's hard experiences with the forces of nature, it is likely their assumptions would more often fall in with the former interpretation.

And yet, oddly enough, as the lights on the prairie continued to be observed into the 20th century, the religious explanation did not last. In the early 1900s, the "ghost lights," as they came to be called, entered the canon of local folklore. None of these tales were about God shining a message, whether terrible or glorious, on bewildered homesteaders. These lights were not divine messages. Rather, they were the lost souls of the Plains Indians whose way of life was lost forever in the massive onslaught of settlers, soldiers and fortune hunters from the East. While they were alive, their souls were connected to the land, but the land was changed when the homesteader settled on it. And so they were cursed to wander without rest, ghost lights looking for a familiar place in the world they once knew. So the tale went. Sightings of the lights continued well into the 1900s, attracting the attention of those who study phenomena of all kinds.

The phenomenon of mysterious lights appearing in the night is not isolated to southeastern Colorado. As it turns out, scientists and paranormal enthusiasts alike have documented similar lights appearing from the forests of Michigan to the swamps of Texas and Florida. There have been myriad hypotheses, ranging anywhere along the traditional spectrum of paranormal theory: strict rational explanation on one side, psychic impressions and spiritual conjecture on the other. Rationalists call luminary phenomena such as these "earth lights," and they have brought up the possibilities of swamp gas, mineral deposits reflecting light and electro-magnetic energy. Others continue to emphasize history and the possibility of unhappy or traumatized spirits manifesting themselves as glowing orbs.

If there is any truth to the supernatural theory, then it seems as though the spirits in southeastern Colorado may have finally found some peace. It has been years since any lights have been spotted there. Indeed, those surviving accounts of the lights have been passed on from previous generations, a fact that has led some people to conclude that these lost souls have finally come to terms with the brutalities of the 19th century. Have the travesties been forgotten? Have the lost souls found peace? It is a nice thought.

A Gravedigger No More

With long, sinewy arms, he cut into the earth, digging by a solitary lantern propped against a tombstone. It was a cold winter's night, and above, the clouds moved across a cruel crescent moon, a curved silver dagger that looked sharp enough to draw blood. It was an empty threat, however, for down below, there was no blood to be drawn— not from the rows and columns of gravestones jutting like bones from the earth, not from the corpses buried beneath and not from the bent old gravedigger, who was as hard and bloodless as the tombstones around him.

Few people in the town of Trinidad could say for certain when he had begun to dig for the dead in the old cemetery north of town. A number of grandfathers claimed they could remember the gravedigger before him, but these men tended to be so old that their judgment in such matters was considered suspect. By appearances, the gravedigger was easily as old as the eldest grandfather in town. But unlike most of the others his age, he rarely said a word to anyone. He was not the type to rant about the times he had seen or pontificate about how much things had changed and about how kids no longer respected the elderly or the traditions they lived by. He did not bother to dole out wisdom, either. He was husband, father, brother or uncle to no one. He was alone, and he was as silent as the graveyard he tended over.

Living in a decrepit old house at the edge of town, he never entertained guests, and the only time he was seen on the street was when he was going for groceries. The only person he ever spoke more than two words to was the grocer, who was almost as old as the gravedigger was. It was said the two men had been friends when they were boys.

The gravedigger was the sort of man who liked to avoid the living. Maybe it was this disposition that pushed him into his line of work. And maybe it was this disposition that compelled him to do most of his work after dark, when there was no one there to disturb him as he went about his somber business.

Which takes us back to what he was doing on this winter night, digging the grave of another Trinidad resident who was likely younger than he. A hard wind was blowing across the cemetery, but the man did not notice. He labored bare-armed, indifferent to the biting cold, the strain of the dig and the dead body in its coffin lying just yards away. He had long grown numb to his work's necessities. For him, all of it amounted to nothing more than peace and quiet—blessed peace and quiet, away from all the busy striving and moiling in town. He was alone here, the only living man in this garden of death, and that's just the way he liked it. With blank eyes and numb arms he dug, just grateful for the stillness, the silence, the lifelessness.

There was a stirring, then, a movement in the corner of his eye. He groaned unconsciously when he noticed it. *Can't they just leave me alone?* he thought. *All these people clamoring for their hopes and ambitions. They've all got something to say. They all want something.* All he wanted was peace and quiet, to be left alone to do his work, but apparently, that was too much to ask. Even here, in a cemetery, at such an hour, they could not let him be.

He did not look up from his digging, but he could see from the edge of his vision that two figures were moving across the graveyard about 20 or 30 yards away. Such was the old man's irritation that at first, he chose to ignore them. He put his head down and stabbed his shovel into the earth, grumbling to himself about who in their right mind would choose to spend their evening going for a walk through a graveyard. *To spite me*, he thought. It was the only reason he could come up with. *A pair of hooligans coming out to torment the crazy old gravedigger. That must be it.*

It struck him, then, that maybe it was not the wisest thing to ignore this pair; two people sneaking into a cemetery past dark were something to be suspicious about. Maybe they even intended to do him harm. *Just let them try it*, he thought. *Digging one grave already, see no harm in digging two more.* He smiled at this—smiled because he hated people. Incompetent, bumbling, troublemaking fools. He hated them all.

Straightening up, he tightened his grip on the shovel and looked across the sprawl of tombstones. There they were: two figures moving across his cemetery. He approached them, looking to cut them off to ask them what they thought they were doing. It had been a long time since he had bothered speaking with anyone besides his friend, the grocer, but he was ready now. They were making him angry, these two, and he was going to do something about it, even with the end of his shovel if he thought it was necessary.

As he approached, however, his anger began turning into something else. Who were these two? Both dressed in long robes with pointed hoods pulled over their heads, they walked through the cemetery with lurching, almost mechanical gaits, making strange crackling noises as they went. When the gravedigger got closer, he saw that their robes were dirty and torn, one a threadbare black, the other a grimy white with a blood red cross emblazoned over the chest. But it was more than their outlandish clothing. The pair were freakishly thin. Their robes hung loosely around impossibly emaciated frames, and he could see the shape of their collarbones jutting from underneath their garments.

The old man slowed down; he was now a mere 10 yards away, holding his shovel in shaking hands. "Hey there!" he called out, his resolve betrayed by his wavering voice. "What d'you two think you're doing in here?!" The two figures continued on with their jerking gait, not even slowing to acknowledge the question. "I'm talking to you!" the gravedigger shouted, now quickening his pace despite his shaking legs. "These are my grounds, damn it! You can't just come in here at this hour, stomping around like you own the place!"

At this statement, the figures froze. They stood unnaturally still, looking like macabre statues draped in cloth that whipped and snapped in the wind. There was dread in the air—glimmering from the sickle moon, blowing in with the frigid wind. The old man stood there, wielding his shovel as though it were a spear, but he was so frightened that he could hardly hold it straight. Goosebumps tickled the back of his neck and ran up and down his bare arms.

The two figures turned to face him—slowly, inexorably, with terrible purpose. The old man's heart leapt into his throat. He saw their hands, their jaws faintly visible beneath their cowls—bone without flesh. Skeletons. *Impossible*, he thought. *Aint' no way.* But they raised their hands to their hoods and pulled them down, revealing two grinning skulls to the gawking gravedigger. There were two skeletons walking through his cemetery.

Then the old man heard a voice in his head. It was a deep and powerful voice, and he knew it was them; they were speaking to him. *These are not your grounds, old man. Not yet. We are the walking dead, and these are our grounds.*

The gravedigger shouted. He dropped his shovel and shouted. He shouted at the top of his lungs, clutched his head in his hands and turned and ran. He ran straight out of the cemetery, leaving behind the half-dug grave and the coffin that was waiting to be buried. He ran from the cemetery and kept running until he reached the home of the grocer, his one and only friend in Trinidad. The gravedigger pounded on the grocer's door, waking him from sleep. And when the grocer came to the door, bleary-eyed and surprised, the gravedigger fell at his feet, blubbering. "I'm through with digging graves in that godforsaken ground," he cried to his lifelong friend. "I'm a walking skeleton and I ain't even dead yet!"

Shocked, his friend had no idea what to make of the blubbering plea, but he did the only thing he could think of at that hour. He offered the gravedigger a job stocking shelves.

The prostrate old man was ecstatic. "I'll take it!" he shouted through grateful tears. And so it was that Trinidad's surly gravedigger became an even surlier grocer. Yet though the tightlipped old man stuck to his anti-social ways, he never again longed for the quiet of the old cemetery. He never ventured back for the rest of his days, and before he died, he insisted that he not be buried there. "I've spent too much of my life there already," he croaked. "I'd rather go someplace new, if it ain't a bother."

5
Modern Mysteries

The Basement

"I bartended for two years while I was going to school," says this Denver engineer. "Made pretty good money and met a lot of people. It got to be a bit of a pain around exam time, but it was something I'd definitely do again if I got the chance." Out of respect for his privacy and the reputation of the bar he worked at, he shall be given the pseudonym "Eric Ward." And as he says, "It's probably best that I not name the place. It's a popular restaurant, and I don't know how they'd feel if it got out that one of their ex-bartenders was talking about how he was sure there was a ghost in their basement. I'm sure I'd come across looking kind of crazy. Or else end up making someone over there angry."

Of course, Ward is prudent to be guarded about these details. There is something that happens to a locale once it is associated with paranormal activity. Even if such claims prove to be specious, talk of ghosts has a way of sticking. Ghost enthusiasts out there have lists of every place that has ever been said to contain spirits. These supernatural catalogues end up lasting for years, defining the paranormal landscape of cities, states and whole countries. Ward is not too eager to see the restaurant he bartended at put down on one of these lists. Nor, for that matter, does he want to become known as the bartender who became uneasy about his job because he was scared of the ghost in the basement.

"There were only three reasons I had to go down there," he says. "I'd change into my uniform at the beginning of the shift. If I had to restock bottles, the booze room was down there, and whenever the taps ran dry, that was where the kegs were. So it wasn't like I had to *work* down there or anything. But I got so I avoided it as much as I could. It sounds pretty pathetic, I know. You've got this fully grown man inventing excuses to get teenage busboys to run downstairs and change kegs of beer. I wonder if any of them were on to me."

They might have been, for Ward is quick to state that he was not the only one who talked about how creepy the basement was. "The guy who was definitely the most vocal about it was Conrad, the dishwasher," Ward says. "Conrad was a middle-aged Chinese guy who didn't speak English too well, but he had no issues telling you about how he hated going down there. If you'd ask him why, up front, he'd tell you straight—because there was a ghost."

It just so happened that the employee who was most vocal about the purported presence in the basement was the one whose job called on him to go downstairs most often. "It was between the busboys and the dishwasher, but I'd say the dishwasher was the one down there most often. If he needed more soap, he'd have to grab it. If the kitchen needed more pots, plates or anything else, it was up to Conrad. They had that guy running down there six, seven times a night. And he hated it. He *totally* hated it."

Ward believes that Conrad must have sensed that they shared this discomfort, because he never failed to talk to the bartender about the basement whenever the opportunity presented itself. "Like I said, he didn't speak the best English, but I'd go back there for more glasses or ashtrays or something and he'd point downstairs and say something like, 'Basement no good. Problem downstairs, eh?' It never got much deeper than that. There was a serious communication barrier up, so we couldn't really get into it. But really, what could you say? There was bizarre stuff going on down there. And neither of us wanted anything to do with it. I knew exactly what he meant by 'problem downstairs.'"

The former bartender describes the basement—large and dingy, with two change rooms set off from a cavernous storage room by a long hallway. The liquor room was behind a locked door right off the big storage room. It was in this big storage area where the "problem" seemed to reside.

"The lights were always off in that room," Ward says. "I used to think they kept them off to conserve energy, but then I figured out where the switch was, and I realized that the lights didn't work. Either the bulbs were burnt out or the circuit was fried, but there was no way to turn the lights on down there. As far as work went, it wasn't an issue. There was no reason, really, for them to be on. Mostly they stored extra chairs and tables in there, and if the busboys needed to get at those, there were always enough of them right around the lit-up hallway so they didn't actually have to go in there. Lucky them."

Not so lucky for the bartender, however. "Whenever I needed to stock up the bar, I had to go right in there," Ward says. "The door was against the wall about halfway in, and the only light I'd have was from the hall. Allow me to say, it was never a pleasant thing to do."

Stumbling past the stacked tables and chairs to jab a key into a locked door in the darkness was one thing, but it was the darkness itself that was the main concern. "The light from the hall was just enough so that you could find your way to the liquor room door, but when you looked deeper into that storage area, it was plain spooky. You couldn't help but get this feeling that there was something in there."

It did not stop at vague feelings, either. From time to time, something in the darkness moved. "The first time it happened, it was a busy night and I had to run down there to get some rye. We were in the middle of a rush and I was moving pretty quick. The spookiness in that room didn't even cross my mind when I was opening the door, but I heard it when I was shutting it behind me." Ward explains that it began with a noise, a shuffling sound from somewhere in the big room. "I spun around to take a look and I saw it. I'm not sure what it was, but it looked like it could have been a person—or more like the outline of a person. It was too dark to see anything clearly, but I got the impression that it was a man, a black outline of a man that was a bit on the big side, maybe six feet or something. I saw him for a few seconds; he was moving really fast deeper into the room and then he was gone."

It happened so fast that Ward asked himself if he imagined it. "That time, I wasn't sure what happened. I was really getting slammed upstairs and my head was all over the place; I had no idea what to think." And yet he did not feel comfortable enough in that dark storage room to stick around to give the matter any thought. "I ran out of there—and when I say ran, I mean I sprinted. When I walked by the dishpit in the back, Conrad gave me this look. He knew I just came up from the storage room and he shot me this 'I know what you just went through' look."

Despite Conrad's difficulties with communication, the dishwasher made sure that everyone knew about how little he liked it in the storage area. "It was one of the jokes among the staff," Ward says. "Every month or so, on any given night, Conrad was bound to have a blowup about having to go downstairs one too many times. When he lost it, you could hear him yelling from the bar, going on about the 'problem downstairs.' It was a good laugh, the look on a cook's face that pushed him over the edge, and there were all sorts of cracks about Conrad and the basement. People got a kick out of it, but I think everyone acknowledged there was some truth to it."

It was silent acknowledgment, however. "No one was walking around talking about the ghost in the storage room. It wasn't like that. But every now and then people talked about how there was something weird about it. Or you'd get someone talking about how they never spent any more time than they had to down there. Me and Conrad, though, our work made it so we were always running down there. It's where our bond came from. We were both dealing with the same thing."

According to Ward, what they were dealing with was not simply limited to uneasy sensations and the occasional rustling movement in the storage room. "Strange stuff happened down there all the time," he says. "Bottles moved around on their own all the time. Never in front of me, but if I grabbed a few bottles then turned my back to grab something else, when I went to pick up the ones I'd just put down, they'd be on the other side of the room. I learned pretty quick not to turn my back on bottles of booze."

More than once, Ward found himself locked out of the liquor room after momentarily placing the keys on one of shelves and then having the door slam shut on its own, trapping his keys inside. "That was another lesson," he says. "Always keep the keys in my pocket. It was embarrassing the number of times I had to go up to some manager and ask him to unlock the bar door because I locked myself out of the liquor room again. And no, the door didn't swing shut by itself, so that was no excuse."

And he did not even attempt to tell anyone what he was really going through. "'Yes, excuse me?'" Ward snorts. "'Can you help me with my keys? The ghost locked me out of the booze room again.' It wasn't an option. I was in no rush to be the other crazy. Conrad could make noise about it, but I wasn't about to commit social suicide."

And so Ward continued working at the restaurant. Barring the occasional conversation about how creepy the storage room was, he said very little about his experiences. "I only worked there on the weekends," he says, "so it wasn't like it was always on my mind or anything.

I never tried to get to the bottom of it. It became something I learned to live with. Besides, there were some shifts where I'd go down there a bunch of times and nothing would happen. It wasn't constant."

Conrad, however, was not able to handle it so well. "The guy ended up quitting in a huff," Ward says. "It was a busy Friday night and he left right in the middle of the shift. No one saw him again. That was it. This isn't such an uncommon thing with dishwashers. It's a really hard job, and the people that do it can be volatile personalities. Our general attitude was, 'Well there goes Conrad. He always was kind of a crazy.'"

But Ward knew better. "I asked the kitchen staff about it after that shift, and apparently he had his last blowup when one of the guys asked him to go down and grab a batch of side plates. He started shouting about how he'd had it with going down there and that was it. He left."

Then, as now, Ward had nothing but sympathy for Conrad. "You know, to get to that stuff, that guy had to grab a flashlight and go right to the back of the storage room. I was having a hard enough time in the booze room, which wasn't even halfway in. Who knows what he was seeing back there? I couldn't have done it either."

Strangeness in the basement aside, Ward has fond memories of his time in the restaurant and frequents it today. He is greeted as a friend and always receives a drink on the house. But every now and then, as he is enjoying the food, drink and company, he remembers the events in the basement, and he remembers Conrad. "A few times, I've come close to asking if they ever got a light working down there, but then it always seems too strange to ask. Maybe all I'm waiting for is the right opportunity." Until then, Ward will have to be content with guessing what was in the basement and whether it is still there.

Only During Storms

In many of the existing narratives of supernatural phenomena, there is usually some measure of causal theory regarding the source of the haunting. It is usually a history traumatic enough to account for whatever bizarre things are said to be occurring. Disembodied footsteps in the hallway of a creaky old house? Perhaps the former owner had lived his entire life within those walls before dying alone in his bedroom. The cold spots and inexplicable feeling of dread in the kitchen of some other home? Storytellers will be sure to bring up the domestic violence that once wracked the household, violence that culminated in a murder in that same kitchen. Homes built over Apache burial grounds, unhappy former residents of homes replaying their traumas from beyond the grave, strong-willed individuals who died with unfinished business—there is no shortage of explanations for why the spirits of the dead choose to haunt the living.

And then there are other cases where it seems that there is no explanation whatsoever, where bizarre events befall a building or its occupants all of a sudden, out of nowhere—sometimes isolated incidents, occurring once and once only, other times continuing, even seeming to get worse with time. The following account, set in one of Denver's outlying areas, presents just such a case, where bizarre phenomena began to plague a home without apparent cause or warning.

"My wife and I moved in in the mid-nineties," begins our witness, who wishes to remain unnamed. "It was our first house, a starter home, not the kind of place we were planning on settling in permanently." A starter home at first, but circumstance has a way of confounding even the best laid plans, and a few years later, this Denver resident found himself in the wake of a divorce, now alone in his one-time starter home.

"She and I were pretty level headed about the situation," he says. "Both of us were after a minimum fuss situation, and I got the place after buying her share out on a loan. There were no problems that way. The whole thing made financial sense, and I'd gotten comfortable there. I didn't want to move. It was a good setup."

While acknowledging that he was fortunate to have had such an amicable divorce, he cannot help but wonder whether the event was somehow responsible for initiating the queer events that began shortly after. To this day, it is the best explanation he has. "Besides the way we started going at each other near the end of our marriage, we'd never had anything remotely weird go on in that house before," he says. "On top of it, it wasn't exactly the sort of place you'd think about if someone said 'haunted house.'" Hardly the looming Amityville archetype with the sagging roofs and swinging shutters, our witness' home looked about as harmless as current suburban architecture can get.

"As far as I know, nothing out of the ordinary ever happened there," he says. "The place was just over 20 years old, bungalow-style set up, sort of a boring place, really.

Not the kind of house you'd look twice at." And yet events after the divorce suggest that there were some far-from-typical forces at work in this typical suburban bungalow.

"I can't say for sure how long it was after she left," our Denver resident says. "I think it was in mid- to late May, somewhere between a month and a month and a half after my ex moved out." He is not clear on the date, but he remembers the evening well. "It'd been a really hot day, and the storm clouds were looking really bad by about five-ish. The sky was getting seriously dark when I was driving home from work."

A certain intangible tension in the air often precedes storms, but according to our witness, the feeling in his house when he arrived was hardly intangible. "I felt it right away. I'm talking pretty well as soon as I opened the door," he says. "It was this cold feeling that just grabbed my guts and spread from there. All of a sudden, all I could think was that there was something in my house that didn't want me there. Really, it was one hell of a scary thing, to be in there. And I had no idea why."

Fighting off feelings he did not understand, he entered his house, walking slowly, cautiously, trying to ignore the fear in his gut and the hairs rising on his arms and neck. "When I think about it now," he recalls, "it was like I was breaking into someone else's house or something. Like I didn't belong there." For reasons he could not explain, he was sure there was someone else in his house, and as he made his careful rounds, it was with the expectation that someone might be lurking around the next corner.

"I was so spooked that when I got to my room, I actually pulled my baseball bat out of my closet before I went downstairs." A thorough search rendered his fears unfounded. "I went on a second tour through the place to be sure," he says. "That time, I even shouted into some of the rooms before I walked in, threatening to call the cops if there was anyone around. I had all the lights on and went through every room. I looked in all the closets, too. And there was nobody."

Still, the feeling that he was sharing his space with some powerful and unfriendly presence persisted. "If anything, I got jumpier after I knew for sure that there was no one there," our witness says. "There was something wrong, I knew it, I could feel it with this ice-cold feeling that wouldn't quit, but it was impossible to put my finger on it. It was like I wanted to get the hell out of my place, but I couldn't say exactly *why*." And so he ended up staying put.

Making an effort to ignore the cold anxiety gnawing away at his insides, he went into his living room to turn on the stereo before entering his kitchen to make dinner. "I remember that I'd just put the can of chili on the stove when it started to come down," he says. "It was a serious storm, and it came down all at once, falling hard right off the bat. Loud enough that it was pretty well drowning out the stereo in the living room."

A spectacle of a storm, but one that the Denver man was not in any shape to take in, for with the pounding rain came something else—a dreadful sensation far worse than before. He makes it clear that it had little to do with the cacophony outside, the rain pounding against his roof, the thunder. It was the *presence* again, the thing he had felt when he had walked in, but now it was somehow bigger; the sense of hostility was more tangible. And, as our witness swears, far more terrifying than it was when he walked in.

"That first time was totally nuts," he says. "I guess it took me by surprise, just how insanely cold it could get in there. How much *force* this thing had. It's hard to explain what it felt like. I mean, strange as it sounds to say that the house was alive, that's the best way to put it. Like the *house* was breathing, fuming, unhappy as hell that there was this guy in its belly."

A smell filled the house, then, an acrid ozone smell, as though a match was just struck. "My legs were telling me to get out, and I almost did, even though it was raining cats and dogs outside." Instead, he called out into his house once again. "I know it sounds stupid, but I was just standing there swearing out loud, daring whatever it was to come on out. At that point, I don't know what I was thinking."

Regardless, he got his wish. A figure flashed across the hall into the living room, and a moment later his pot of chili was flying across the kitchen. "Things get kind of muddy after that," our witness says. "I wasn't really thinking straight. I know for sure I was pretty freaked out— pretty well like anybody would be. I grabbed the wooden spoon I'd been stirring the chili with and went running out to the living room."

The living room was empty when he got there. "But the second I stepped in, the stereo went full blast. I mean, I actually *saw* the dial *physically* go up to 10 all by itself, right in front of me. Scared the living hell right out of me, like I jumped so hard that my head pretty well hit the roof." The moment he found his composure, he ran across the room and turned the stereo off. He recalls: "I hit the power button and pulled the plug out of the wall, too. Just to be sure."

But whatever was roaming through his house wasn't finished with him yet. "I was probably standing there for about 10 seconds, 20 max, when I heard hell breaking loose in the kitchen," he says. "That, for sure, was when things started to get clearer. I mean, I was still wound up bad, but it was pretty clear to me at that point: there was something in my house. Something I couldn't see. And this thing seemed pretty intent on screwing around with me."

It was with more purpose than panic, then, that our witness strode back into his kitchen, bracing himself for whatever was causing the ruckus within. "By the sound of it, I was thinking for sure it was going to be bad in there," he says. "It still surprised the hell out of me, though." No wonder. Most people would consider moving out if the bedlam was half as bad as he describes. "Basically, everything was everywhere. I mean, all the cupboard doors were open, and pretty well near half of them were cleared out. I'm talking pots and pans on the floor, broken plates. Same with the drawers. My forks, spoons and knives were all over the place. The chili I'd been cooking was all over the wall. Total mess."

But that was it. Whatever had made this mess was nowhere to be found, while the only way out was through the back door, which was locked, as he had left it. "At the time, it was a bit too much to deal with," he says. "I mean, whatever made the mess was obviously still in the kitchen. There was no other way out. But there was nobody there." Nothing he could see, anyway. After hollering a string of epithets into his kitchen, he grabbed his keys, got into his car and drove to the nearest fast food establishment. "I made sure that was the last time I tried cooking when there was a storm coming."

That was the essential connection. Returning later on that night after the storm had subsided, the rattled Denver resident was relieved to find that the foreboding feeling he had felt in the house was there no longer. "The mess was still there, but it was pretty clear to me that whatever had been there before was gone."

How did he know? "I just knew. The cold wasn't there; the feeling in my gut wasn't there. I didn't have that feeling walking down the hall that someone was going to jump out from behind a corner and clobber me. Plain and simple, it was my place again."

And so it remained for the next little while, as the spooked resident tried coming to terms with what had occurred. He admits that the casual manner with which he speaks of the incident today belies the difficulty he had with it at the time. "For sure, it really freaked me out back then. Even though everything *felt* right again after that storm, I had serious problems trying to get comfortable in there again. I mean, this thing took over my home when I was right there. It was like it was making it clear who *really* ran the show: that being *it*, not me. You go through something like that, home doesn't feel like home anymore."

Then again, it has been said (and will be again) that time heals all wounds, and, in this case, it certainly did the trick for lingering apprehension. Although he was not able to forget the event, time quickly took the edge off the fear. The next week and a half passed without further incident, during which time he had already stopped obsessing over the existence of ghosts. Was it possible? Apparently so. Could he actually have one in his home? So it would seem. But was it actually possible? And so on. "The strangest thing was that I'd been there for years already and no issues. Then the ex takes off and *bang*— I've got Casper's angry brother messing around with my stereo and making a mess in my kitchen."

Bizarre as it was, after little more than a week these questions became less pressing, and he began to think that the whole thing may have been a one-time event. That was until another rainstorm erupted over the Denver sky. "Yeah, the second time was way worse than the first," he begins. "I think mainly because it was in the middle of the night when it happened."

Claiming to be a heavy sleeper, he goes on to say that he woke later on that May to the sound of the rain pounding on his roof. "Sure, it was loud, but not so loud that it would wake me up," he says. And then he felt it. "When I felt that cold in my stomach, I was up in a sec. It was the exact same feeling as before, and it hit me right there that it wasn't the storm that got me up. *It*, whatever the hell *it* was, was back."

He was not lying there for long when a crash sounded from the kitchen. It was the same sound as before, the crash of his cupboards and drawers being emptied. "There were a few seconds when I was lying there thinking that maybe that would be it. That it'd stop there, and then it got crazy again in the kitchen."

There was no doubt in his mind that he was dealing with his phantom resident, but he still grabbed his baseball bat on his way to the kitchen, hollering threats at whatever was there. "Yeah, I was pretty sure that there was nothing there to hit, but I was shouting anyway—when you're scared as hell, you've got to get it out of your system somehow."

The incident concluded much the same way it had the first time. The crashing ceased the moment he switched on the light in the kitchen. On the floor was half of his kitchenware; the room was empty and the rain was pouring against the windows. "That was it. That time, the cold gripping at my gut cut out as soon as I was in the kitchen. It didn't end up driving me out of the house. So, I guess you could say things were a little better the second time around."

Nevertheless, though the cold presence had departed, the night had lost none of its menace. "The storm passed pretty quick after that," says our witness. "I mean, I was still standing there looking at the kitchen floor when the rain stopped—it couldn't have been a few seconds, tops, after the place got back up to a normal temperature."

Not having the energy to clean up that night, he kept the kitchen light on and went back to bed. "I knew for sure that it was gone, but that didn't help things that night. My mind was playing all sorts of tricks on me. I'll just say that it was a hell of a thing keeping my eyes open at work the next day."

Jumping at bumps and shadows through the wakeful night, he was able to make the obvious connection between the two separate incidents: they both occurred during rainstorms. "I'll tell you, that totally changed the way I looked at the weather reports," he says. The next forecasted rainfall came later on that same week, with showers predicted through the course of the day.

"I took a look before work that morning, and it was looking pretty dark out," he says. Thinking about the mess that might be made in his kitchen if he was not there to stop it, the Denver resident took precautions: "I duct taped the entire kitchen. Every cupboard and drawer in the place—sealed it all shut. I also disconnected my stereo and my TV. Made the place as ghost-proof as I could," he says, laughing.

It rained on and off that morning, and he was preoccupied with the state of his house throughout the day. All the way home, it was the one thing on his mind. He was relieved, to say the least, when he got home and discovered that his kitchen was still intact. "I never really thought the ghost-proofing had much to do with the fact that my place wasn't trashed," he says. "You know, if this thing could throw open pretty well every drawer and cupboard in the place and dump everything into the middle of the room in a few seconds, I'm sure it could've taken the duct tape off first."

Sound reasoning, which leads us, then, to the inevitable question: why? If the man's house had been ransacked in the previous two storms, why had it not done the same while he was at work? This Denver resident has had years to think about it, and has an answer ready: "This thing wasn't some random supernatural force of nature set loose in my house. It was doing this, wrecking my place, for a real reason. It was trying to *tell* me something."

And he had a pretty good idea what this "something" was. "It made its first appearance almost right after me and my ex settled with our divorce," he says. "We had a good split, neither of us had gotten too emotional about the whole thing. I guess to the point where it was definitely kind of weird. It was like we both knew that there was nothing left, and wanted to end it together. Totally mutual." Or so he thought.

Putting together the incidents with the recent departure of his ex-wife, he decided to make plans to see her. "I didn't say anything about what was going on," he says. "She's a practical, hard-headed sort of person who'd get pretty weirded-out if I called her up out of the blue and told her what was going on." Without any real idea what he was going to say, he set up a coffee date for that weekend.

"Well, I found out things weren't going exactly like I thought," he says. "After we talked for a bit, she told me that she'd been feeling really bad about what happened. Not just about us. She said she was having some withdrawal issues with not living in the house anymore. She only realized how attached she'd gotten to it after she moved out." Not only did he feel a certain sympathy for his ex, but he was also quick to link her separation anxiety with what had been going on.

He admits it was a far-fetched theory, but it was the only one he had. "I'd read somewhere that poltergeists often showed up in the same houses that unhappy teenagers lived in, and there was this theory that the strong negative emotions in these houses could show up as poltergeists." Formulating his own theory on what might be happening in his house, he wondered if his estranged wife's emotions were somehow responsible for the angry energy he was encountering.

"I had no idea if it would work or not, but it became a real priority for me to get her to feel better about the situation," he says. "Looking back, I think our break was *too* easy. Even though we were both reasonable about it, she never got a chance to really say 'bye' to the place."

Couples have their complexities, and our witness does not bother going into his. Whatever their issues, he had reason to believe that more time together would meliorate the unspoken difficulties between them. "I invited her over a few times for dinners and lunches. She really appreciated it, and it was good for me, too. Not that we talked so much about our marriage and what went wrong, but we still sorted it out, in a way. Even though we never had too much drama between us, there *were* bad feelings. And I'm pretty sure we managed to clear them up. Or most of them, at least."

The Denver resident's feelings were vindicated in early June, when a storm broke one weekend while he was having lunch at home with his ex. "Wouldn't you believe it? Nothing happened. No cold. Nothing messing with my stereo, and nothing wrecking my kitchen either."

It wasn't simple. Even after he and his wife had reconciled their undeclared differences, bizarre, if somewhat less dramatic, events continued to occur in the home. "It went on for a few years after that," he says. "Nothing like before, but still enough to make me think, *All right, there's still something going on here.*" He goes on to list the phenomena that persisted, always when he was alone during storms—the doors that would gently swing shut on their own, the flickering light in his living room, the way his kitchen appliances would mysteriously change location when he had his back turned. "Up until I moved out last year, whenever there was a storm, I always got that same feeling, like I'm not alone."

So although this Denver man may have been partly correct in his assessment of the mysterious force haunting his home, there were still things going on that he never fully understood. "Who knows?" he concludes. "I've got no idea if the people that live there now are still dealing with it, or it left when I did. My gut still tells me it had something to do with me and my ex, but in the end, it was really just a hunch."

Apparition at Pike National Forest

"I've lost track the number of times I've been out biking at Pike," says a Colorado Springs mountain bike enthusiast, who, requesting anonymity, shall be called "John Lucas" in the following account. "When I first moved out here, me and my work buddies made it out at least three times a month. There's some of the best cross country trails I've ever ridden up there, and biking them mountains is a hell of a novelty when you're a guy who's grown up in Michigan."

John admits that though he's unabashedly into the outdoors, he was never the sort to dwell on the countryside he enjoys so much. "Yeah, it was the same way back in Michigan," he says. "My parents had a lakefront place, and I guess I more or less grew up looking at the whole place as a playground. We had our jet skis out on the lake, and when my brothers got me into rock climbing, mountainsides turned into these radical challenges. I'm not the kind of guy that sits back at a mountain pass and goes, 'Look at that, why don't you.' I'm on a great vantage point, and I start thinking if it's possible to base jump off it."

So it was that this self-confessed adrenaline junky did not bother to think much about the places in which he enjoyed his outdoor pastimes. Having always linked the outdoors with recreation, he did not have it in him to ponder the significance or the beauty of the landscapes that he had always taken for granted.

For John, Pike National Forest was where he and his friends took their bikes for some off-road riding, but he knew nothing of the land he was riding through. He did not know that Pikes Peak was named after Zebulon Pike, the first explorer to record his journey through the region. Nor did he stop to think that the stunning peaks and valleys his bike trails wove through were once home to Native people. Indeed, the verdure and rock he so regularly rode through had once been a battleground between the mountain-dwelling Ute and the Arapaho and Cheyenne, who roamed the plains.

That was until one weekend in May 2002 when John was out with two of his friends, tearing their way over some tricky single track deep in the woods beneath Pikes Peak. "It was our usual routine," he says. "We left the day before and car-camped the first night so we could get up early the next day and start riding right away. We'd ride all day Saturday and most of Sunday and then pack up and be back home before dark."

"I'd ridden with those two guys a hundred times before," he continues. "Sometimes we'd get a few more guys out with us, other riders came and went, but us three had been riding it pretty constantly for about two years, then." In those two years of good riding, during which they had had their share of wipeouts and wildlife encounters, never once did any of them experience anything out of the ordinary—nothing that would lead them to think there was anything wrong or unnatural in those woods.

"I remember it pretty clearly. We were moving pretty quick up this steady ascent that was cluttered with a lot of rocks and roots," he says. "It wasn't that hard going, but it was tricky enough that you had to pay close attention to what you were doing. It was late morning, a good sunny day, and we'd been riding for a few hours already—about three hours—and I remember looking at my watch and thinking we'd be breaking for lunch pretty soon."

It happened not long after he checked the time. "I can't say for sure, but it couldn't have been 10, 15 minutes tops after I shouted back that it was almost time to break," he says. "We'd been on that trail before, and there was this part where it turned and then dipped into this shaded stretch of ground that went on for 20 to 30 yards. It was always cooler down there than on the rest of the trail—being shaded and all." (It is interesting that John automatically offers the rational explanation for the cold on that part of the trail, even after what he experienced there.) "So yeah, I just made the turn and dipped in, picking up some speed on the descent. I was under the trees, about halfway through, when it hit me all at once…" John pauses here, silently reliving the memory.

He continues, now in a more cautious tone. "It was crazy, really hard to explain," he says. "The best I can do is that it felt like someone was reaching in and pulling the breath right out of me. Like, I'm on my bike moving along, everything's fine, and then I can't breathe. I mean *not a single breath*. And then, right around that exact second, I'm, like, *freezing* cold. I said it was always a bit cooler in there, right? This was something different. This was crazy cold. I'm talking it's May and I can see my breath in front of me."

John pauses again, thinking carefully before continuing. "I should probably say that it all happened really,
really fast. I know what I saw and everything, but every
now and then, when I think about it, the *order* gets mixed
up. I'm not a hundred percent sure if the cold hit me
before the breath was sucked out, or it was the other way
around. Maybe they both happened at the same time.
That's not what made me shout, though. Sure, I couldn't
breathe, but my bike was still moving. My legs were still
going. I didn't know what the hell was happening, but I
still had my eyes on the trail."

That changed when, from the corner of his eye, he
spotted the shape moving alongside him among the
shadows of the darkened wood. "Right then, if I had any
breath in me, I'm pretty sure I would've screamed," he
says. "At first I couldn't make out what it was, but then I
could see that it was the shape of a man. I'm not saying
it was a man, 'cause there was no man there—it was the
shape of a man, a big, black shadow without a body to
cast it." And this shadow without a body was moving fast,
matching his speed as he rode, coming at him out of the
trees.

"It all happened super fast after that," he says. "I
remember there was a second where I was thinking, *No
way. This can't be happening. I'm seeing things.* Then it was
right out of the trees and right beside me." John explains
that it was only up close and in plain sight for an instant,
but it was so surreal in that split-second that it was seared
into his mind forever. "I couldn't make it out so clear
when it was in the woods, but it was a hell of a trip to

see it once it was out on the trail. It looked like a solid shadow of this huge guy who was over six feet tall and crazy-built." When John describes the figure as a "solid shadow," he means to say that where features should have been, there was nothingness. No face, no clothes, no hair—just a deep, black emptiness.

"I only got to see it up close for a second. It came straight at me, and didn't slow down for a second. I was still pedaling when it hit—or not really *hit*. Actually, I think he went straight *through* me." When it happened, John claims that no physical impact came with the collision. Instead, he was overcome by the sense that he had been immersed in frigid water. "Then everything was black, and that was it."

The next thing he remembers is waking up with his two friends kneeling over him. "I was lying in the middle of the trail when they found me," he says. "I guess my tires were still spinning when they took the turn and saw me face down on the ground. They told me I wasn't out for more than a few minutes when I started coming to."

The moving shadow was the first thing that came to mind the moment he got his bearings. The second thing that came to mind was how it might not do for him to break into a terrified tirade about what he had just seen. "The first thing out of my mouth was, 'Did you guys see anything?' But I got one look at their faces and figured out pretty quick that I wasn't too keen on going any further with it."

Still, his riding partners had missed the fall and were full of questions. "The trail was pretty easy—flat, not technical at all," he says. Picking himself up and noting that he had gotten away with just a few minor scrapes, John muttered that he must have blacked out. "They thought that was pretty funny," he says. "You know, ribbing me about how if I was going to start fainting 'cause the rides were getting too tough, that we could tone them down a bit." John laughs. "That's just the kind of guys they are."

Nevertheless, he opted for the teasing over the truth. He continues: "I was nowhere *near* telling these guys what I saw. This was the craziest thing I'd ever seen, right? We got on our bikes and kept going, but my heart wasn't in the ride anymore. The trees were looking different. I jumped a few times 'cause I was sure for a second that I saw something moving in the forest. I couldn't get rid of this feeling that something in there was watching us." John's friends noticed how rattled he was, and the trio went easy for the rest of the day. "Definitely, I'd never been so happy to be back at the campsite," he says.

And yet this relief did not last. It did not take long for John to realize that the uneasiness on the trail had followed him back to where they had pitched their tents. As subsequent events later that evening would prove, whatever had come at John Lucas was not done with him yet.

For their Saturdays after the ride, the tradition was to get a little unwound with the help of a few bottles of beer. That night, however, John needed more than a little unwinding. "I think everything felt different right away— like, as soon as we got off our bikes. I couldn't get my head around it, and it's a strange thing to try and explain, but it had to do with this feeling in the air, even the way everything looked."

John speaks here of what can only be described as a prevailing disconnect with his surroundings, a sense that the place they were returning to was not quite the same as the place they had left, even though, of course, nothing had ostensibly changed. He was having problems focusing on immediate distances; at times, he imagined that the trees were slowly revolving around their campsite. "The spinning wasn't the worst of it, either," John says. "Every now and then when I'd concentrate enough on the woods, the whole scene would get kind of wobbly, like everything was underwater."

These episodes never lasted for more than minutes at a time, but they were enough to throw John off. "I started thinking that maybe I knocked my head on that fall," he says. "The thing was, it wasn't just the way things looked. The weirdness went further than that. For one, I couldn't get warm enough that night. I built up the fire super-high and put on long pants and shirt, but there was this deep cold—it was like I was freezing from the inside."

Things only got worse as the night wore on. John goes on: "I was trying to ignore it and get into the conversation and all. But the guys could tell I was out of it. And I don't know if it was contagious or something, but they started to feel weird, too. It started to get real quiet. It was like we were all on the same weird trip, like we were all quiet because we were listening for whatever was out there."

John claims that as they sat there around the fire, trying to appear nonchalant about the darkness folding in around them, they all *knew*; somehow they knew something was out there, watching them. It would not be long before the night confirmed their suspicions.

"It was sometime past 10 o'clock and we were talking about going to bed when we heard movement in the trees." John laughs when it is suggested that if every group of campers hearing movement at night thought *Ghost!*, every campsite across the country would be haunted. "Sure, there are all sorts of things out there that scurry around at night, but this was different. I knew it, because the feeling I was getting was exactly what I felt earlier, when the shadow came out at me. The guys knew it, because I could see it in their faces. They were pretty damned spooked."

One of John's friends tried making a joke out of it, saying, "I'm not going to even ask if you guys heard that." They laughed and tried to shrug it off as a shuffling nocturnal creature, but a pall had been cast over the evening and the conversation was half-hearted. They finished their drinks and called it a night.

But if John thought he would get any sleep once he retreated into the safe confines of his tent, he was dead wrong. It was all on account of the thing he glimpsed by the dying embers of the fire—the shape of a man, a shadow, blending into the night's darkness, so that he was almost invisible. "He, it, was just standing there, looking right at me, and that cold got colder, and it got hard to breathe."

This time, he called out to his friends. A reflexive "Guys!" escaped his lips, and his riding partners turned to him. "What?"

But then he blinked and it was gone. He did not sleep a wink that night.

It's years later, now, and John Lucas still has no idea what he experienced on that trip. While the trio have biked Pike National Forest numerous times since then, he says they maintain a largely unspoken aversion to the campsite they stayed in that night. For his part, John has never told his friends what he saw on the trail, not even as a possible explanation for the uncomfortable night that followed.

He laughs as he gives his reason: "Trust me, I'm not about to go on record as the guy who fainted and fell off his bike because he saw a ghost."

The First Day of School

"We'd been living in that house for something like three years when it started to get crazy," she says. "Before that, there was nothing going on there that'd get me thinking we'd moved into a...I don't know...a place that was *haunted*." This Denver mother pauses here, taking a moment to think before continuing. "I should probably say that's as far as *I* was concerned. I hadn't noticed anything out of the ordinary. But then I suppose I can't have been noticing everything that was happening." She pauses again, laughing now at something she has just told herself. "Okay. It's a tough thing for a mother to say, but now I *know* I wasn't noticing everything that was happening." Especially, it must be added, when these "happenings" relate directly to her child.

Agreeing to tell her story on condition of anonymity ("more for my children's sake than mine"), she shall go by "Janice" in the following account. Janice has two children. Her son is the eldest, nine years old at the time of this writing: "His father's boy—busy, a bit too impulsive with a bit too much energy, but he's getting there." And there is her daughter, a happy, healthy, imaginative child of six years, who Janice had once spent an inordinate amount of time worrying about. The reader may ask, here, what exactly constitutes an inordinate amount of time when it comes to a mother worrying about her children. Well, Janice's case was a little bit of an exception.

"My baby girl has a serious imagination," Janice says. "When my son's out in the yard chasing balls around and lording over the other children, my girl's sitting down with a book or setting up a house and happy family with all of her stuffed toys underneath the dining room table. She's got no problems being alone. Give her a bunch of books and her stuffed toys, and she'll keep herself busy for practically the whole day." Janice recognized this trait early on in her daughter's life; perhaps, she adds today, a little bit too early.

"We moved into our last house about five years ago, when my son was four and my daughter was just a one-year-old. It was a bigger place," Janice says. "We moved in mainly because it was a nice neighborhood and it was bigger than our last. We thought we'd need more room with the latest addition to the family."

The house was not new, but neither was it very old. It seemed to have a typical enough history. "They told us the first couple that moved in there were seniors. The wife died of a heart attack, and the husband stayed on there for a little by himself before he moved to a seniors' home. But of course my husband and I didn't really give this any thought. And anyway, to this day, I'm not sure if that had anything to do with what went on. It's just the closest thing I've got to an explanation."

Janice continues: "It was about a year after we moved in when my girl started talking to herself after I put her to bed—maybe for 10 to 15 minutes when it happened, baby talking to herself until she fell asleep. At least I always assumed that was what was happening." Certainly this was a safe assumption. Who else would the toddler be talking to after her mother left her in her room by herself?

"There were times when I could hear her babbling away so loudly that I would go back and check in on her, thinking maybe her brother was in there causing mischief," Janice says, "but it was her in there by herself. I'd open the door and she'd see me and start laughing away—happy kid."

Happy and healthy; Janice did not even think to ponder her child's nightly babbling. "I did tell friends and family about it, and people always laughed," she says. "Who knows why babies do anything, right?" Today, however, she is sure that there was something else going on— that her daughter was talking to someone, or something, after Janice turned out the light.

"The talking never really stopped," Janice continues. "Her vocabulary got a lot better over the next year. She was making a lot more sense. I'd gotten used to it by then, and never really stood around and listened to her for too long after I shut the door. It'd usually start with her laughing, and then she'd start counting up from one to ten and then make up numbers after that. I never really stuck around to hear what she'd say after that, but sometimes I could hear her from downstairs. She was usually asleep in about 15 minutes."

Janice still remembers the first time she asked her daughter who she talked to at night. "I'll always remember it because of the way it made me feel when I heard it," she says. "She laughed and said that she was talking to the

Hairy Lady. It's not like I believed her for a second. But it still gave me a bit of a chill. Where would she have gotten that from? The Hairy Lady. None of her books had anything about a Hairy Lady."

Janice asked her daughter where the Hairy Lady came from. "She told me, 'Mom, she comes out of the closet.' She was laughing about it, so I didn't think there was any problem. I never had an imaginary friend, and neither did my son. But I figured if you had one that made you laugh, then there probably weren't any problems, right?" Still, it made Janice uneasy when her daughter divulged another detail about the Hairy Lady. "She told me how funny this Hairy Lady was. It made her laugh that she came out of the closet crawling like a baby."

Janice laughed along with her daughter at this, but claims that right after breakfast that day, she went up to take a quick look through her daughter's closet. "It got to me for sure, this Hairy Lady talk," she says, "but I took a look and, surprise, surprise, there was no Hairy Lady crouched in my daughter's closet."

The next year passed without incident. "A few times after she told me about the Hairy Lady, I stood by her door and listened. She'd always start laughing. Once she said, 'Stop, that tickles!' Another time, she was saying something about chocolate ice cream, her favorite." Several times, Janice walked in on her daughter in the middle of these exchanges, but always found her daughter alone.

"I asked her those times, when I barged in like that, if the Hairy Lady was around because I heard her talking.

She told me, no, she wasn't, because she got scared and ran away." That settled it for Janice. Her daughter had an imaginary friend. She picked up this "Hairy Lady" business from either the television or something she had heard from her brother. Then it was the first day of pre-school, and everything went to hell. "We ended up moving out in mid-November, about a month and a half after school started," Janice says. "That was how bad it got."

Janice returned home from dropping her daughter off that morning and was immediately aware that was something was wrong. "We've got a little dog, a Jack Russell, and as soon as I opened the door she came running up to me, whimpering and whining, and not in a happy-to-see-you kind of way. She was bowed down low; it was obvious she was scared out of her wits."

Also, it was Janice's habit to leave the radio on for her dog when she was out of the house. Although the radio was still on, it was turned to a different station than she had left it on, and the volume was far too loud. "I had no idea what to make of this, because I'd activated the house alarm before I left, and nothing had triggered it," Janice says. "It crossed my mind that my son might be in the house, fooling around. But it didn't make sense that he would cut school because he was looking forward to it so much."

Confident that there was no one in the house, Janice reached for a rational explanation. "I told myself that the dog probably knocked the stereo, which made the station change and the volume go up, and scared the hell out of her." Shutting the door behind her, Janice walked to the radio, changed the station back, turned down the volume and then went to the kitchen to have her breakfast.

"There was only one strange thing that happened when I was eating," she says. "It was a minor thing, but I'll never forget it." Janice had just sat down and started eating, newspaper in front of her. "I didn't look up from my paper and reached for the glass of OJ I just put down, but it wasn't there." More than a little alarmed, Janice shot a glance around the kitchen. Her glass of orange juice was on the counter across from the island where she was sitting.

"Now *that* got to me," she says. "I *knew* I'd just filled that glass and carried it to where I was eating. I *knew* I saw it when I started reading. It was simply impossible that I'd imagined the whole thing." And yet, remarkably, Janice was able to reason out what had just occurred, a fact that speaks volumes to how firm the prevailing rationalism of our age is in our minds. "Yeah, I got spooked, but the glass was on the other side of the kitchen, right? So that's where I must've left it." She laughs. "Everyone knows that glasses full of OJ don't just move around by themselves."

But when Janice went upstairs to make her bed, she came face to face with an event that even she would not be able to explain away. "With everything that ended up happening, I think what I saw in that bedroom was the scariest. Or allow me to qualify that: when I realized that my daughter was involved with what was going on, my *concern* with everything peaked. But to this day, when I think about that morning, I still feel it."

Janice continues: "By then, everything was fine. I don't think I was bothered in any way about the radio, my spooked dog or the fact that my glass of juice moved across the kitchen by itself. Crazy as it sounds now, I didn't feel strange or scared and I didn't have goose bumps or anything. There was no warning at all."

Janice had the duvet off the bed and was spreading the sheet when she laid eyes on her daughter's imaginary friend for the first time. "I was unfurling the sheet on the bed, and when I saw the shadow against the white, I almost had a heart attack." The black outline on the white bedspread told of a short, stocky figure on the other side of the sheet. That was all Janice was able to register before the sheet came down and she was staring at the Hairy Lady, no more than six feet away.

"I screamed. I had no idea what to think. Right there in my bedroom there was this—I don't know, *woman*. She was the most hideous thing I've ever seen. She was about five feet tall or so with big shoulders; she was wearing this black dress and her skin was peeling and dirty. Her hair was black and long and braided in clumps, and she also had these thick long hairs sprouting from her chin and nose and all around her eyes. The worst, though, was the way she was looking at me. She looked so *angry*, with these hateful black eyes. She looked like she wanted to kill me."

Janice's first thought was that she was about to be attacked. There was an intruder in her home, a hideous, gnome-like intruder who was going to attack her and abscond with her belongings. But the moment it occurred to her to turn around and run from her room, the woman in black vanished. "When I say vanished, she didn't jump out the window or duck under the bed or anything like that. She just disappeared—there one minute, gone the next. My bedroom was empty, like she was never even there to begin with." Then Janice noticed the closet for the first time. Neither she nor her husband had opened the closet that morning, but the door was wide open. That was when it hit her for the first time. She had just seen her daughter's imaginary friend: the Hairy Lady.

"The first thing I thought about was my poor girl, and how all this time, when I was thinking this Hairy Lady was an imaginary friend, she had this *thing* in her room every night." With the realization came an urge to immediately go and pick her daughter up from school. "Right then, the only thing I could think was how I never wanted to let her out of my sight again."

That feeling passed, however, as Janice's prevailing rationalism took over. "I put a few things together pretty quickly," she says. "First of all, I gathered that this woman I saw and the Hairy Lady that was visiting my daughter were one and the same. This was the first time she showed up in front of me, and it was also the first day I sent my daughter off to school. The Hairy Lady was angry at me." Over the next few weeks, she would come to know exactly how angry the Hairy Lady was.

"The best way I can describe it is that that house became a battleground," Janice says. An apt metaphor— the fight escalated daily between the two equally determined combatants. Janice made the first move.

"I knew she wasn't going to be happy when I insisted that my daughter sleep in my room that night," Janice says, "but after I saw what I saw, there was no way I was going to let my baby sleep in the same room with *that*." Janice's husband thought it curious that his wife was insisting their daughter sleep between them, but accepted his wife's explanation that she had felt a sort of separation anxiety on their daughter's first day of school. "I wasn't about to tell him what was really going on," she says. "It's the kind of thing that I would have no idea how he would react to. He has a high pressure job, and I can only imagine what he'd say if one day he came home and his wife told him, 'Honey, there's a hideous Hairy Lady living in our daughter's closet!'"

Her daughter was happy about the novelty of sleeping in her parents' room, but the Hairy Lady was definitely not. "I wasn't surprised when my daughter came up to me at breakfast and whispered in my ear that something bad had happened in her room, and she thought the Hairy Lady was upset. I waited until everyone was off for the day before I went up and took a look. She was right, the Hairy Lady was definitely upset."

The bedroom was a disaster. It looked as though the closet had exploded, its contents scattered all over the floor. Her toy chest had been plundered as well; dolls and stuffed toys lay on the floor amid the clothes. "That morning I discovered something positive about being angry," Janice says. "When you're angry, I mean really, really angry, it makes it hard to be scared." Instead of being afraid that the Hairy Lady might turn up again,

Janice found herself hoping it would happen. "No matter how creepy the stunted little thing was, I was good and ready to tear a strip out of her for making that mess."

Perhaps it was a good thing, then, that the Hairy Lady did not show herself that day, leaving Janice alone with her anger as she cleaned up her daughter's room. "After I was done, I went out and bought a lock and chain. That night, I got my daughter to sleep with us again, and I locked her closet shut."

The strategy did not work well. Not only was Janice's husband starting to wonder about his wife's insistence that their daughter sleep with them, but the next morning, she found the lock unfastened and the closet door wide open. There was the same mess for her to clean up. And that was not all.

"That third day, she really wanted let me know what she could do," Janice says. "After she messed up my daughter's room, she waited until I got back home and then she visited the kitchen." Her experiences in her kitchen would be far more dramatic than they were on the first day. Today, Janice is able to laugh about it. "She was in the mood for a bit of showing off, that's for sure."

It began as it did on the first day. After Janice had dropped off her daughter, she went home to have breakfast. "I think I was expecting something to happen," she says. "I was getting the feeling already that things were escalating, and she definitely didn't let me down that day."

With one eye on her newspaper, the other on her glass of orange juice, Janice began having her breakfast. "The move-the-glass trick was already old hat," she says with a laugh. "This time, she went for the do-the-dishes-the-quick-way trick." Sitting at the edge of her seat, Janice jumped when the taps on the kitchen sink spun on their own, and water started streaming out of the faucet. Before she could get up, her family's breakfast dishes began lifting themselves out of the kitchen sink and, one by one, throwing themselves against the wall on the other side of the room.

"Okay, now that *really* made me angry. I'm not too proud of the things I ended up shouting then. I don't know if I've ever been so upset. I thought about the way she looked, and I went on a complete name-calling rant. It was like I was in primary school all over again. I was in the kitchen shouting that nobody likes hairy ladies, especially ones that look like trolls. I told her that a monster like her had no place around my daughter. None of that stopped her, though. She kept going until every plate and glass in the sink was smashed—more mess for me to clean."

The Denver mother began to recognize the futility of her situation soon after that. "It really became a question of what I could possibly do," she says. "You've got this mostly-invisible Hairy Lady in your house that is angry because you're sending your daughter off to school. I can't see her, except when she wants me to. I can't reason with her or touch her. She's got all the power in the situation. But of course I'm not about to pull my daughter out of school just to make her stop."

Over the next few weeks, Janice exhausted herself trying to come up with a solution. "I came up with all sorts of theories." Thinking that the Hairy Lady's manifestation might have something to do with where her daughter was sleeping, she had her change bedrooms with her son. But the Hairy Lady had no problem with the change, and the first night the young girl was in her new room, Janice heard her talking again.

"All that time, I didn't feel comfortable confronting my baby about the Hairy Lady. I felt as though if I talked to her about it openly, it would just re-enforce its presence in our lives. I think I was still in denial." In the end, it was Janice's daughter who brought up the Hairy Lady with her mother.

"I think it was in her second week of school," Janice says. "Things were still getting progressively crazier. By then, I'd gone on three separate trips to get new kitchenware that had been smashed, cleaned my daughter's new room every morning since she'd slept there, and was having a difficult time trying to convince my husband that I wasn't crazy."

Intent on keeping the appearance of the Hairy Lady as quiet as possible, she found herself at a loss for words when her daughter approached her about the matter. "I suppose that since she'd known about it for so long, she might have understood that I was carrying it around now, as well. We were in the car after I picked her up from school when she told me, 'Mom, the Hairy Lady is angry.' I was shocked. It was the biggest thing going on in my life then, but I wasn't ready to hear someone, that being my daughter, talk about it. It was unsettling to me how matter-of-fact she was about it."

Janice had done her best to keep all signs of the Hairy Lady's obvious discontent invisible to the rest of her family. Although her daughter had seen the mess in her own room on certain mornings, Janice made sure that the rest of the house was in good order before anyone got home. "I asked her what made her think that the Hairy Lady was angry, and she said because the Hairy Lady told her. She told her that she wasn't happy that I was making her go to school in the morning, and it was making her angry that I was trying to keep them apart."

Janice knew she had to handle the situation carefully. "I asked her if she liked the Hairy Lady. She thought about it for a few minutes before she said that she *used* to like her because she made her laugh, but that she wasn't so sure anymore. She wanted to go to school, she said, because she wanted to be smart like her brother, and she didn't like it that this thing in her room was getting angry about it."

Later that week, Janice decided to get outside help. "The goal was to get this thing out of my house as quietly as possible," she says. "I went to a priest first, thinking maybe a few quick prayers would help. He was visibly disturbed by what I told him, and was pretty adamant on the point that he didn't believe in ghosts, and suggested that I might need to see some help. Can you believe it?" Janice laughs.

"I managed to convince him to come on over, and I managed to get him to bless our house. He wasn't so formal about it. He basically went into every room and said a prayer. I managed to get him to say two prayers in my daughter's room. I could tell he thought I was nuts." Despite the priest's prayers, the Hairy Lady made another appearance later on that night. "The holy angle didn't work," Janice says.

She tried more worldly methods next. "I did a little looking around on the internet, and was surprised to find quite a few groups who investigate this sort of thing. The first group I called showed up with a lot of equipment. There were four of them. They set up audio recorders all over my daughter's room and kept a camera on the closet. They rigged the kitchen up the same way. They took photographs of everything in sight, checked the temperature in my daughter's room every five minutes or so. One of them claimed she was a medium. She asked me a million and one questions about what was going on and then walked around the house with her eyes closed—trying to get in tune with the energies or something."

As thorough as the group was, Janice confesses that she could not get herself to put much faith in them or their methods. "It looked like they had their hearts in the right place, I won't take that away from them," she says. "But as much as they were trying to be professional, it was pretty clear to me that they didn't have any experience with what I was going through. They *wanted* to help, but they were more about collecting evidence for themselves, and personally, it seemed like their methods weren't working too well for themselves. They gave me a sample of what they considered to be solid evidence from their other investigations, and it wasn't too impressive. I don't want to sound cruel, but I saw a hairy little woman standing there in my bedroom, and these people were showing me photographs with little white blurs and static on tape."

She was even less impressed with the second investigator she called in. "She was a one-woman show," Janice says. "And after she took a look around, mumbling a little hocus pocus in my daughter's room, she turned around and started blaming *me* for the Hairy Lady. This woman was full of bizarre pseudo-psychological theories, about how the Hairy Lady was a paranormal manifestation of my subconscious fear of seeing my daughter grow up and leave home." Janice laughs. "She said something along the lines of—the only way for me to beat the Hairy Lady is to learn to let my daughter go! Can you believe it? She's four years old, going to pre-school for half a day, and there's some woman sitting in my living room telling me I have to learn to let her go."

That was it for the outside help. Janice came to the conclusion that she would have to deal with the Hairy Lady on her own, and there was a time when she was determined to be the one who came out on top. Then came the night when her daughter woke her up in the middle of the night, and all that changed.

"She snuck into our room in the middle of the night and woke me up quietly," Janice says. "I knew right away that it had something to do with our unpleasant guest, and I took her out to the living room before I asked her what was wrong. She said that the Hairy Lady was scaring her. My attitude did an about-face right there. My impression had always been that the Hairy Lady and my daughter got along. *I* was the one she had a problem with, not my baby. That was when I realized that winning this war against this thing wasn't worth it if it was affecting my daughter negatively in any way."

Janice asked her daughter what the Hairy Lady had done to frighten her. "She told me that she grabbed her wrists hard and told her that something bad would happen if she kept going to school. She said that this Hairy Lady told her that she was different now that she was going away in the morning, and that she didn't like who she was becoming."

That was essentially it for Janice. Making a mess and throwing things around the kitchen were one thing, but threatening her daughter was something else altogether. "The next day, I told my husband we were moving out. I didn't tell him the real reason. We still hadn't sold our previous home, and it was between tenants. I insisted that I was happier there." Janice laughs. "It sounds like a lot to ask, but my husband had never been able to say no to me."

So concluded Janice's confrontations with the Hairy Lady. "Nothing out of the ordinary happened when we were moving, and as soon as we started packing, my daughter said that she stopped getting the visits. I guess she must've known that the game was over." When Janice is asked why the Hairy Lady would have accepted their move so quietly, given the reaction when her daughter started going to school, the Denver mother is only able to speculate. "Who knows? I think it was obvious she was attached to my daughter, and maybe she didn't want to leave things on a negative note. Whatever the reason, that was the last we ever heard of her. She didn't move back with us, and its been years since my baby girl's said a word about her. Thank God."

The Garage

"What can I say, Bruno's been there forever," says this Denver resident, whose sense of humor comes through when he talks about the ghost in his parents' garage. "I've known about him since I was a kid. Hell, I was the one who gave him his name in the first place. It stuck. I guess so did he. Seems crazy, but he's still there, hanging out in my parents' garage. And to think people used to give me grief about staying in my parents' basement into my late 20s. God knows how old Bruno is. The guy's gotta move on, already."

Going by the pseudonym "Brian Cobb," this eyewitness to the supernatural has long since moved out of his parents' home, though he says he keeps in touch regularly and visits about twice a month. "My mother still talks about him every now and then—like, 'Oh, Bruno's such a dear. The other day, your father left the garage door open and Bruno shut it all on his own when it started to get dark.' So yeah, he's helping around at the house. Good ol' Bruno. It wasn't always like that, though. My mom used to be scared silly of him."

The Cobbs moved into their Denver bungalow in the mid-1970s, when Brian was nine years old. Today, he claims that he knew there was something going on from the very beginning, while at the same time confessing that memory is not always such a reliable thing. "I can't say for sure. I'd like to think that I was on to Bruno from the start, and when I remember it, it always felt like there was something off about that garage. I can't think of a time back then when that garage felt normal, but then I obviously can't say I can recall *every* time I was in that garage." He pauses. "I'll just say this, even before Bruno started taking care of my bike, I'm pretty sure that there was something fishy going on in there."

Although Brian admits he cannot recall with any certainty the first time he *sensed* there was a presence in his garage, he has no difficulty telling about his first encounter with it. "We'd been there for less than a year," he begins. "It was the summer break, and I'd been spending a lot of time with this group of kids who were really into biking—off-road biking. I guess you could say we were a little ahead of the time. It was the 1970s, and there was no such thing as mountain bikes yet, but we'd head out with these beat-up old 10-speeds and tear through the local walking trails like little demons. Tons of fun," he says.

As much fun as it was, the bikes they took on these rides were hardly built for riding off-road, and they took as much of a beating as the boys who rode them. "That was part of the fun," Brian says, "how completely out of control we were. Ripping over tracks on these flimsy little things. When you're a kid, you can smear yourself over a trail a hundred times on a ride and not pay for it the next day. Yeah, there were tons of wipe-outs, and those bikes got beat up real bad, real quick."

Brian says it was about a week and a half into the summer, and he had already been on five rides. "It was my dad's bike and it was smashed up good. I didn't know anything about bike maintenance besides oiling the chain, and I was pretty lazy about that, too. So I was in this situation where my dad was going to lose his mind as soon as he noticed how trashed his bike was. It was a good thing that Dad didn't notice a lot, even back then."

He recalls with confidence that it was late in the morning, either Tuesday or Wednesday, and he walked into the garage to get his father's 10-speed. Incredibly, he specifically remembers that it was their sixth outing. "I'll never forget the way my dad's Nishiki looked," he says. "The last time I left it there, it was a mess. The front tire was bent to hell, the drive train was covered in mud and the rear derailleur only worked on the middle three gears. If my dad knew the kind of damage I was doing to his bike, he would have lost his mind. But he was away in Houston for business for a lot of that summer and barely even looked at that bike. I think it's still in his garage, and he's probably only ridden it once or twice since I left." Which is a shame, considering how well Bruno has taken care of it.

"Yeah, I don't know what I thought when I saw it there. First off, it was up on its kickstand instead of lying on the ground where I left it. The drive train was cleaned right up and shining like new—it'd just been oiled. And what really blew my mind was when I got on it, I saw that someone tightened the spokes so that the front tire wasn't wobbling anymore." Incredible as the cleaning and oiling of the drive train were to the young boy, the straightened tire was especially hard to buy because he knew that his father did not own the proper tools for such a job. "Forget the fact that there was no one at my place who knew how to straighten a tire, we didn't even have the tools you need to do it!" He overcame his shock to take the tuned-up bike for a ride, but has never forgotten the incident. From then on, he was certain there was something in the garage.

"Maybe you'd have to be nine years old to be able to accept something like 'there's an invisible bicycle repair-man in my garage,' and not have it slow you down too much. But hey, this invisible guy in my garage—because who else could it have been?—he fixed my bike! That was one supremely cool thing to do. This guy, whoever he is, he's my pal!"

Bruno received his name soon after that. "Of course he needed a name. This guy wasn't just making sure my dad's bike was okay to ride. That was just the start. He also helped keep the place clean, helped us find missing tools, stuff like that."

Brian was not the only one in the family who realized that there was something going on in the garage. "No, I didn't tell my mom anything," he says. "She figured it out on her own. There's only so many times you can go to grab the mop bucket to do some cleaning and find it already full of soapy water, ready to go, and not start to wonder." Being a nine-year-old boy who was painstak-ingly developing his own notion of cool, he was reluctant to let his parents in on his discovery, and he was not sure what to do when his mother approached him about it.

"That was before I realized that me and my mom were on the same side," he said. "She was a lot like me. Dad always had his head caught up in work and who knows what else. Even when he was around, he wasn't really. But my mom saw things. She got what was going on, and

Bruno became the thing we had in common." Yet as helpful as Bruno was with the chores, Brian's mother found
it far more difficult to accept him than her son did. "She
was scared at first, that's for sure," Brian says. "She didn't
think it was nearly as cool as I did."

Certainly many people would be able to relate.
Discovering that there is an invisible presence in one's
garage is a difficult thing to wrap one's head around, no
matter how helpful that presence is. "Maybe the problem was that Bruno wasn't just about helping around
the house," Brian says. "Sometimes in the middle of the
night you could hear him banging around in the garage.
It wasn't anything too nuts. It was this deep and low thud,
like something heavy was falling against the rafters in the
garage over and over again. It was just loud enough for
you to get up and wonder, 'What the hell is that?'"

It did not help matters that this thudding only
occurred when Brian's father was away. "It was kind of
a reverse situation," he says. "My mom would come to
my room, all nervous-like, and ask me what I thought
about the noise. I'd laugh it off, tell her it was all right,
that the guy in the garage was a cool guy. Maybe he was
horsing around or something." A number of times, Brian
crept downstairs to the garage to see if Bruno was actually stomping around. "Really. How cool would it have
been to actually *see* the guy banging around down there?"
Yet he never was. In fact, when Brian opened the door a
crack to take a look, the banging stopped—every time.
"Whatever his reasons are, Bruno's a low-key kind of guy.

I lived 20-some years with him, and never saw once what he looked like."

He was not so bashful in other ways. The lights in the garage were known to flicker on and off on certain evenings. When the family installed a garage door opener, the device acquired a habit of coming to life on its own; for the first few weeks after they purchased it the garage door regularly opened and closed, though there was no one at the switch. Brian and his mother were relieved when Bruno lost interest with the new appliance. "It's not cool to have your garage door opening on its own in the middle of the night," he says. "When I think about it now, I can relate to my mom not wanting to go in that garage by herself. But at the time, I never got it. Bruno was my buddy, and that was it."

Even though mother and son spoke openly with each other about the presence in the garage, for the first few years Brian kept to himself the name he had given it. "I'm not sure how much sense this makes, but it probably would've been easier on her if I would've let her in on the fact that I gave him a name earlier. I remember how hard she laughed when I told her the name I gave him." According to Brian, it was right around then that she began to relax about the goings-on in the garage. After that, Bruno was what they had in common. It was the inside joke that they kept from Brian's perpetually absent-minded father.

"Bruno could be a riot, that was for sure," Brian says. "He really got off on messing with my dad. Harmless stuff. I don't know how many times Dad came into the living room telling us the keys jumped out of the car door again. The 'running keys,' he called them. He never actually saw them run with his own eyes, but if he had them in the car door and looked away for a second, they wouldn't be there anymore. He'd end up looking all over the place before he found them. They'd always turn up in some obvious place, too, like on the backseat, in the ignition or on the hood. Poor Pop; I'm sure there were times when he thought he was losing his mind."

Yet as mischievous as he could be with Brian's father, Bruno never did anything that was remotely dangerous. Indeed, as Brian affirms, there were many times when Bruno saved Brian's dad from himself. According to Brian, his father and heavy machinery did not go well together. "When my dad took on woodworking projects, Bruno made sure he didn't screw up too bad and hurt himself. I know you're asking yourself, what kind of harm can a guy do building bookshelves and birdhouses? Well believe me, my dad had a way of making a lathe into a deadly weapon, never mind what he could do with a band saw. If it wasn't for Bruno, I'm sure Pop would've lost a few fingers, at least."

Brian continues. "We got used to having him around. I grew up with this invisible dude living in the garage. I went through all sorts of stages with old Bruno," he laughs. "I remember times when I was a kid, going to the garage and telling him that he didn't have to say in there. You know, he was welcome inside the house, if he wanted." For all Brian knows, his ghostly friend may have taken him up on the offer. He could not see him, after all. But neither Brian nor his mother was ever given reason to believe that Bruno entered their home. Never once did anything out of the ordinary occur within the house. Bruno had a strict garage-only policy.

"I think when I was about 11 or 12, I started wondering what Bruno's story was," says Brian. "You know—why was this guy in our garage, anyway? Did something happen in there? When that movie *Poltergeist* came out, I was convinced that our garage was built over an Indian burial ground. You're curious, right? After a bit of time, you start taking him for granted, but then every now and then, it hits you all over again. We've got a ghost living at our place. This is crazy. I went through a phase when I talked to him all the time, but he never said a word back or gave me any kind of sign that he heard me."

Brian never got any answers; Bruno's provenance remains a mystery to this day. "I gave up communicating with him a long time ago," he says, "and my mother, I don't think she's ever said so much as hello in all this time. We both learned to accept him way back. And my dad, well, I'm pretty sure he still has no idea we've got a permanent lodger in our garage."

Ghostly Glossary

ANGELS: Derived from the Greek word *angelos* ("messenger"), angels are the celestial messengers and guardians of a deity; though commonly associated with Christianity, angels are common to many religions. They are immaterial beings, sexless creatures of pure consciousness that possessed a knowledge no mortal could ever even hope to comprehend.

CLAIRAUDIENT: An individual with the ability to perceive sound or words beyond the range of hearing. These sounds can come from outside sources such as spirits or other entities. Clairaudience is said to be a form of channeling messages through audible thought patterns.

COLD SPOTS: Commonly associated with haunted sites, a cold spot is said to result from a ghost absorbing the necessary energy to materialize from its surroundings. They are usually quite localized and are 10 or more degrees cooler than the surrounding area.

DEMON: In Christian theology, demons are the instruments of evil, the fallen angels cast out of heaven with Lucifer. They exist for no other purpose but to torment and torture the living through abuse, assault and possession. However, in other cultures, demons are not nearly so malicious. To the Greeks, daimons (translated, the word means "divine power") served as intermediaries between mortals and the gods of Mount Olympus.

ECTOPLASM: A term popularized in the film Ghostbusters, ectoplasm is said to be a white, sticky, goo-like substance with a smell resembling ozone. It is, hypothetically, a dense bio-energy used by spirits to materialize as ghosts. Its existence has never been proven.

EMF: An electromagnetic field, or EMF, is associated with an electric charge in motion. Many paranormal researchers equate an EMF with paranormal activity, believing that ghosts generate high levels of electromagnetic energy through their activities.

ESP: Extrasensory Perception, or ESP, describes the ability to perceive and receive information without the use of any of the usual five senses: sight, touch, smell, hearing and taste. Not surprisingly, ESP is often referred to as the sixth sense.

EVP: Electronic Voice Phenomena, or EVP, is a process through which the voices of the dead are captured on an audiocassette. How the process works is a bit of a mystery, but it usually involves placing a tape recorder at a haunted site. When played back, the voices of the dead should be clear on the recording and should not be confused with background noise or static.

EXORCISM: An exorcism is the purging of a person, place or thing that has been possessed by a demon or other unnatural force. It is normally carried out under the close supervision of a religious official, thoroughly trained and capable.

GEIGER COUNTER: An instrument that detects and measures radioactivity, or the spontaneous emission of energy from certain elements. This device searches for fluctuations in Alpha, Beta, Gamma and X-ray radiation, which point to a disturbance in spirit energy.

GHOST: Derived from the German word *geist* and the Dutch word *geest*, a ghost is the physical manifestation of an individual's disembodied spirit. It may appear as a figure, but a ghost can also manifest itself through smells, sounds and other sensations. At the heart of any belief concerning ghosts is the idea of a separation between the physical body and the metaphysical soul. The body perishes, though the soul does not.

MATERIALIZATION: The process through which seemingly solid objects or individuals appear out of thin air. It was a popular and well-documented phenomenon during the earliest years of Spiritualism, when mediums commonly caused objects like coins and cups to materialize.

ORBS: Though they may vary in shape, color and size, orbs are most commonly round in shape and whitish gray in color and are usually, though not always, found in photographs taken during a haunting or at a haunted site. They are believed to represent the spirit of the dead. Because dust, moisture and lens flare can easily be confused with orbs, some critics have argued that orbs may not be enough proof to legitimize a haunting.

OUIJA BOARD: An instrument that allegedly can be used to contact or channel spirits of the deceased. It is usually a wooden or cardboard device inscribed with the alphabet, the words "yes" and "no" and the numbers 0 to 9. There is usually a slideable apparatus on rotating castors or wheels with a pointer. The operators of the board place their fingers lightly on the slideable device and wait for it to move.

PARANORMAL: Any event that cannot be explained or defined through accepted scientific knowledge is said to be beyond what is normal. It is, therefore, paranormal.

POLTERGEIST: A combination of two German words, *poltern* (to knock) and *geist* (spirit), a poltergeist is characterized by its bizarre and mischievous behavior. Activities of a poltergeist include, but are not limited to, the moving of furniture, the throwing of objects and the rapping and knocking of walls. A poltergeist may also be responsible for terrible odors and cries. Typically, the activities of a poltergeist appear unfocused, pointless and completely random.

POSSESSION: A condition in which all of an individual's faculties fall under the control of an external force, such as a demon or deity. An individual possessed by a demon may alter his or her voice, even his or her appearance, and be fearful of religious symbols.

REVENANT: From the French *revenir* (to return), a revenant is a ghost that appears shortly after its physical death. Usually, it will only appear a few times, perhaps even just once, before disappearing from the earth forever.

SPIRITUALISM: A movement that originated in the United States in 1848, Spiritualism is a religion whose beliefs are centered upon the idea that communication with the dead is altogether possible. By the late 19th century, spiritualism had become popular throughout the United States. Its popularity ebbed in the early 20th century as many of the religion's earliest mediums were exposed as frauds, but rose again after World War I. It is still popular today.

THERMOGRAPH: A self-recording thermometer that traces temperature variations over time.

TRANCE: A trance is essentially an altered state of consciousness in which the individual, though not asleep, is barely aware of his or her immediate environment. There is some speculation that during a trance, the body enters a state that hovers somewhere between life and death, which frees the mind to explore a higher realm and gain spiritual insight.

Lone Pine Publishing International

ENJOY MORE FASCINATING ACCOUNTS OF AMERICA'S PARANORMAL FOLKLORE.

Ghost Stories of the Rocky Mountains Volume 1 *by Barbara Smith*

These haunting tales include mysteries surrounding many well-known buildings and landmarks, some of which people say are inhabited by restless spirits to this day! This collection features stories from the battleground of Little Bighorn, Warren Air Force Base, Banff National Park…and more.

$10.95USD/$14.95CDN • ISBN10: 1-55105-165-6 • ISBN13: 978-1-55105-165-9 • 5.25" x 8.25" • 240 pages

Ghost Stories of the Rocky Mountains Volume 2 *by Barbara Smith*

From the Rocky Mountains come more tales of high-country haunting: the spirits of the many souls who perished during the 1903 Frank Slide are still cleaning up the rocky site; Idaho's phantom white stallion rescues people who have lost their way in the mountains; Colorado boasts a ghostly bookworm that haunts a used bookstore… and more.

$10.95USD/$14.95CDN • ISBN10: 1-894877-21-7 • ISBN13: 978-1-894877-21-3 • 5.25" x 8.25" • 216 pages

Ghost Stories of Arizona and New Mexico *by Dan Asfar*

In New Mexico, a camper at Bonita Lake has a chilling encounter with a mysterious figure in the middle of the night, and a brutal mining accident scars Dawson, a ghost town in the Sangre de Cristo Mountains. In Arizona, a Phoenix resident has a helpful spirit in his new home, and troubled spirits linger in the abandoned Yuma Territorial Prison. Read these tales and more.

$11.95USD/$14.95CDN • ISBN10: 976-8200-15-4 • ISBN13: 978-976-8200-15-0 • 5.25" x 8.25" • 208 pages

Ghost Stories of Texas *by Jo-Anne Christensen*

Along with its Wild West spirit, geographical diversity, dramatic history and sheer size, Texas contains a wealth of spooky stories of the supernatural. Enjoy tales from the Alamo, Big Bend National Park, Dallas, Fort Worth, Laredo, Galveston, Corpus Christi and more.

$11.95usd/$14.95cdn • ISBN10: 1-55105-330-6 • ISBN13: 978-1-55105-330-1 • 5.25" x 8.25" • 232 pages

Ghost Stories of California *by Barbara Smith*

California has a wealth of tales about the supernatural and the folkloric from all over the state: legends such as the ghostly sailors that roam t he decks of the *Queen Mary* at Long Beach, the malevolent phantoms that still haunt Alcatraz and more.

$11.95usd/$14.95cdn • ISBN10: 1-55105-237-7 • ISBN13: 978-1-55105-237-3 • 5.25" x 8.25" • 224 pages

Ghost Stories of the Old West *by Dan Asfar*

Explore the haunted histories of some of America's most infamous gunslingers, lawmen and opportunists, as well as prisons, saloons and forts where the lawlessness of the Old West found its truest expression.

$11.95usd/$14.95cdn • ISBN10: 1-894877-17-9 • ISBN13: 978-1-894877-17-6 • 5.25" x 8.25" • 216 pages

These and many more LPPI books are available
from your local bookseller or by ordering direct.
U.S. readers call 1-800-518-3541. In Canada, call 1-800-661-9017.